ONE UPON A RHYME
- A MUSICAL TALE-

BOOK, LYRICS & MUSIC BY RONVÉ O'DANIEL

BOOK BY J KYLE MANZAY

MUSIC BY JEVARES MYRICK

Uproar Theatrics

LICENSING & PRODUCTION INQUIRIES
Uproar Theatrics, LLC.
hello@uproartheatrics.com I www.UproarTheatrics.com

Once Upon a Rhyme
Book and Lyrics copyright © 2016 by Ronvé O'Daniel
Music copyright © 2016 by Ronvé O'Daniel & Jevares Myrick

Once Upon a Rhyme is published by Uproar Theatrics, LLC
500 8th Ave FRNT 3, #1714 New York, NY 10018

ISBN: 978-1-968051-33-4

First Printing, May 2025

CAST OF CHARACTERS

5 Principle Men
4 Principle Women
5-6 Ensemble (Cyphers)

PRINCE - Protagonist. African American man, 18-22. A gifted classically trained high school dancer and rapper. Nerdy but can be charming. Rapper, singer, dancer, actor. Childish Gambino/Donald Glover meets Chance the Rapper sprinkled with some Andre 3000.

THE MC - African American male mid-30's. Shape shifting, mystical storyteller who narrates the action of the show. Leads the audience on the journey with a secret connection to the story. Rapper who can sing. Chuck D meets James Earl Jones blended with a little Slick Rick.

STACY - Woman, any ethnicity 18-22. Assertive, confident, trendy, brash, influenced by hip-hop culture. R&B/POP singer and dancer, rapper. Ariana Grande meets Cardi B garnished with some Janelle Monae.

DEBORAH - African-American woman, mid to late 40's early 50's. Community college African American studies professor. Strong, assertive, nurturing, no-nonsense humor. R&B singer. Aunt Vivian (the first one) meets Audra McDonald infused with some Whitney Houston.

CHARLES - African-American man, late 40's to early 50's. Works at an auto-factory. Good   looking male who speaks his mind. Passionate, prideful, charming and stubborn. R&B singer. Poetry/ Rap is a plus. Charles S. Dutton meets Gerald Levert, with a splash of Teddy Pendagrass.

GARY - African American man age 30. College dropout with aspirations of being a self-made businessman. Fun, energetic, carefree, slick, charismatic, a hustler. R&B singer and rapper. Fresh Prince meets Jason Weaver peppered with a little Kanye West...the old Kanye West.

SLIM - Woman, any ethnicity, age 30. Gary's friend, works as a young executive for a major hip-hop record label. Responsible, charming, professional but has swagger. Rapper who can sing. Angie Martinez meets Gabrielle Union drizzled with Vivica A Fox.

BIG TREY - Caucasian man age 25. Talented local gangster rapper with an incredible buzz around the industry. Tough, arrogant, lots of "street credibility" Don't get it twisted, he's no "fake thug" - he's the real deal and takes the streets very seriously. Can be rude. Rapper. Machine Gun Kelly meets Meek Mill soaked up in some Yelawolf.

CYPHERS - Dance Teacher, Ensemble, lead narrators. 6-10 young, multi-ethnic, male/female identifying, non-binary rappers and dancers to play Prince's friends, neighborhood residents, Hip Hop Fans and various other shape-shifting characters. Singers, actors, rappers, dancers.

MUSICAL NUMBERS

Act 1

1. Once Upon a Rhyme

2. Jump

3. Prince Rhyme Book Entry 1

4. Magic

5. Real Life

6. Mo iLLA

7. I'm the King

8. Interlude - The Freestyle Cypher

9. Prince Rhyme Book Entry 2

10. Together

11. All I Know

12. Our Own World

13. Happily Ever After

14. No Guts, No Glory

Act 2

15. Interlude - Prince Studio Rap

16. Be Cool, Be Gangsta

17. Spirit of the Thug

18. Interlude - Prince Rhyme Book Entry 3

19. The Truth

20. Interlude - Hip Hop Flashback

21. Hold On, Be Strong

22. Blank Page

23. Pop's Rap

24. Rewind

25. Mo iLLA Reprise

26. Keep It Real

27. This is Your Moment

28. You Are Enough (Finale)

ACT 1

(BLANK STAGE.)

SONG 1: "ONCE UPON A RHYME"

> *(THE MC, holding a Rhyme Book, appears with
> the CYPHERS. He opens the book and begins
> reading. As he raps the CYPHERS accent his
> lines through dance.)*

THE MC
ONCE UPON A RHYME NOT LONG AGO, CITY
OF...

THE MC/CYPHERS
...CLIFFTOWN...

THE MC
IS WHERE WE START THIS SHOW.
A SMALL, MUNDANE SUBURBAN...

THE MC/CYPHERS
...COMMUNITY...

THE MC
LIVED A KID WHO YEARNED FOR...

THE MC/CYPHERS
...OPPORTUNITY.

THE MC
A DANCER BY THE NAME OF...

THE MC/CYPHERS
...PRINCE HARPER!

> *(THE MC motions for PRINCE, who appears*
> *wearing a hoodie and sweatpants, toting a*
> *dance bag. He clutches his rhyme book in one*
> *hand and a pen in the other. PRINCE leads the*
> *CYPHERS in choreography as THE MC raps.)*

THE MC
SINCE A CHILD HE DANCED IN...

THE MC/CYPHERS
...BALLET.

THE MC
BUT EQUALLY GIFTED WITH THE LANGUAGE
AND WORDS,
WRITING POETRY AND RAPS...

THE MC/CYPHERS
...EVERYDAY!

PRINCE
(Writing in his Rhyme Book.)
AS I CONVEY EMOTIONS THROUGH POETIC
EXPRESSION.
IN SEARCH FOR MY PLACE ON THIS EARTH
WHERE I'M ACCEPTED.

> *(The CYPHERS turn their back on PRINCE.)*

PRINCE/THE MC
EIGHTEEN YEARS OLD...

THE MC
...WITH A CHOICE HE'S GOTTA MAKE.
WHILE HIS LIFE IS AT STAKE!

CYPHERS
(Gasps.)

AHH!

*(THE MC motions. THE CYPHERS transform
the blank stage into the city of Clifftown.)*

CYPHER 1
HE'S GONNA NEED ASSISTANCE ON HIS PATH.

CYPHER 2
FACING RESISTANCE...

CYPHER 3
FACING THE WRATH...

CYPHER 4
TAKES PERSISTENCE!

THE MC
A LITTLE MAGIC, HIP HOP WIZARDRY TO LEAD
HIM TO VICTORY.

(THE MC motions PRINCE to step forward.)

THE MC/CYPHERS
WE CAN'T LOSE OUR ENERGY!

CYPHER 1
LIFE OR DEATH...

CYPHER 2
FREEDOM OR JAIL...

CYPHER 3
HEAVEN OR HELL...

CYPHER 4
WE GOTTA SAVE PRINCE FROM HIMSELF!

THE MC
BREATHE:

CYPHERS
INHALE, EXHALE.

(CYPHERS surround PRINCE.)

THE MC
AND GRAB A FRIEND.
THIS IS WHERE THE STORY BEGINS...

(THE MC snaps his fingers and the lights come
up to reveal a birthday cake with a giant candle
that reads: "18". DEBORAH, CHARLES,
GARY, STACY, LEONARD, JJ, and other friends
surround PRINCE. PRINCE stares at the cake
with deep contemplation.)

THE MC/CYPHERS
PRINCE... PRINCE... PRINCE.

<u>SCENE 1:</u> (DEBORAH & CHARLES'S HOUSE.)

DEBORAH
Prince?!?

PRINCE
Huh?

DEBORAH
Did you make a wish?

PRINCE
Yes.

DEBORAH
Then blow out your candles.

>   *(PRINCE takes a deep breath, then blows out*
>   *the candles. Everyone cheers.)*

<u>SONG 2: "JUMP"</u>

GARY
AYE CUZZO!

CHARLES
BOY!

STACY
YOUNG CHEESY!

DEBORAH
PRINCY!

DEBORAH/CHARLES/STACY/GARY/CYPHERS
THIS IS YOUR MOMENT!

                              GARY
AYE CUZZO!

                              CHARLES
BOY!

                              STACY
YO CHEESE!

                              DEBORAH
PRINCY!

DEBORAH/CHARLES/STACY/GARY/CYPHERS
THIS IS YOUR MOMENT!

AS THE WORLD SPINS, AND THE PAGE TURNS,
A NEW CHAPTER WILL BEGIN.
ONE DOOR SHUTS, ANOTHER OPENS UP
AND TOMORROW RUSHES IN.
WELCOME TO EIGHTEEN.
YOU ARE A GROWN UP.
IT'S THE BEGINNING!
STANDING ON THE EDGE: IT'S TIME TO JUMP!

                              GARY
CUZZO!

                              CHARLES
BOY!

                              STACY
YOUNG CHEESY!

                              DEBORAH
PRINCY!

DEBORAH/CHARLES/STACY/GARY/CYPHERS
THIS IS YOUR MOMENT!

GARY
AYE CUZZO!

CHARLES
BOY!

STACY
YO CHEESE!

DEBORAH
PRINCY!

DEBORAH/CHARLES/STACY/GARY/CYPHERS
THIS IS YOUR MOMENT!

THE MC
WELCOME TO THE WORLD OF PRINCE,
AND HIS LIFE ON THE DAILY.
BIRTHDAY BOY, AKA...

THE MC/DEBORAH
"MAMA'S BABY".

THE MC
FINDING BALANCE AS HE HONES HIS TALENTS.
THIS WAS ALSO DEBORAH HARPER'S
CHALLENGE.

DEBORAH

I WORKED EXTREMELY HARD
TO RAISE YOU IN NORTH CLIFFTOWN:
A TWO PARENT HOUSEHOLD, A WEEKLY
ALLOWANCE.
PLEASE DON'T LET US DOWN.
SINCE YOU WERE FOUR YEARS OLD.
I'VE GROOMED YOU TO BREAK THE MOLD.
KEEP ON DANCING:
THAT'S HOW YOUR STORY GETS TOLD.

*(DEBORAH hands PRINCE a box. He opens it
and pulls out ballet slippers.)*

JJ

Whoa!

LEONARD

Are those the new Capezios?

PRINCE

Wow. More dance slippers.

DEBORAH

They're gold! You can shine with your shoes and your
moves! Desmond Conservatory, here we come!

PRINCE

We?

THE MC

EVERY FATHER HAS A DREAM FOR THEIR SON.
WHAT THEY WILL BECOME WHEN IT'S ALL SAID
AND DONE.

WORKIN' ROUND THE CLOCK NON-STOP
TO BE THE BEST FATHER.
THIS IS THE AMBITION OF CHARLES HARPER.

*(CHARLES hands PRINCE a manila envelope
with a bow on it.)*

PRINCE
What is this?

CHARLES
It's the business license for "Harper and Son": our new auto-repair business.

PRINCE
You want me to work for you?

CHARLES
With me.

PRINCE
Fixing cars?

CHARLES
Building a future.

ALL MY LIFE I'VE WORKED TO CLIMB,
RAISING YOU THE ENTIRE TIME.
MAKE YOU TOUGH, DO ALL I CAN.
TURN YOU INTO A MAN.
IT'S BIGGER THAN YOU, BIGGER THAN ME.
THIS IS OUR FUTURE LEGACY.

THE MC

...ON THE GRIND
WITH MONEY ON YOUR MIND.
YOU ALWAYS GOTTA KEEP YOUR PARTNER BY
YOUR SIDE.
BUILD YOUR BUSINESS BY ANY MEANS
NECESSARY.
MEET PRINCE'S COUSIN: THIS IS GARY.

GARY

YO, I READ THE RAPS THAT YOU WROTE.
A BIT ON THE WEIRD SIDE, BUT THEY KINDA
DOPE!
I BET IF WE GET THE RIGHT BEAT,
SHIT'LL SOUND SWEET.
COULD GET YOU POPPIN' WITH A COUPLE
TWEETS.
I KNOW YOU TAKE BALLET CLASS
BUT YOU ARE ONE LEOTARD AWAY FROM
LOSING
YOUR B-L-A-C-K PASS.
YOU GOTTA HAVE A LITTLE MORE SWAG,
SO PEEP WHAT I GOT IN THE BAG.

(PRINCE pulls out a box of Air Jordans.)

PRINCE

Oh. Shoes?

GARY

These ain't just shoes. These are Limited Edition J's, dawg!

PRINCE

But I wear New Balance.

GARY

Well you need a new wardrobe. It's all starts with the kicks.

THE MC

LAST BUT NOT LEAST: A GIRL WITH HER OWN VOICE,
AND ON THE DANCE FLOOR, SHE'S ON POINTE!
MAKE NO MISTAKE, SHE'S
BEEN FOCUSED LATELY
TO REACH HER ULTIMATE GOAL: THIS IS STACY.

STACY

Young Cheesy's finally grown! Here ya go.

(Hands PRINCE a small bag. PRINCE opens it up and pulls out a pair of tights.)

PRINCE

Tights?

STACY

Rip proof tights. To prevent another costume malfunction so you don't leave your partner hanging onstage like you did me.

PRINCE

You're not going to let that go, are you?

STACY

Nope.

ABSOLUTELY NOT, IT'S WHAT I DO!
WHO ELSE IS GONNA BUG THE LIVING HELL OUT OF YOU?
WHAT OTHER FRIEND YOU GOT THAT'S GONNA POINT OUT YA FLAWS?

11

STACY (CONT)
AND EVERY LITTLE THING YOU DID WRONG,
JUST BECAUSE?
THE DESMOND CONSERVATORY'S COMING
IN A FEW WEEKS.
AND WE SUPPOSED TO PICK PARTNERS FOR
OUR NEW PIECE.
WHOEVER YOUR PARTNER IS, GOD HELP 'EM!
THE TIGHTS ARE FOR YOU AND THEM: YOU'RE
WELCOME!

DEBORAH/CHARLES/GARY/STACY/CYPHERS
BREATHE, BREATHE: INHALE, EXHALE.
THIS IS YOUR LIFE.YOU ARE EIGHTEEN.
HOW WILL YOU PROCEED?.
BREATHE, BREATHE: INHALE, EXHALE.
THIS IS YOUR LIFE. YOU ARE EIGHTEEN.
NOW YOU MUST SUCCEED.

AS THE WORLD SPINS, AND THE PAGE TURNS,
A NEW CHAPTER WILL BEGIN.
ONE DOOR SHUTS, ANOTHER OPENS UP
AND TOMORROW RUSHES IN.
WELCOME TO EIGHTEEN.
YOU ARE A GROWN UP.
IT'S THE BEGINNING.
STANDING ON THE EDGE: YOU HAVE TO JUMP!
YOU HAVE TO JUMP!
YOU HAVE TO JUMP!
YOU HAVE TO JUMP!

GARY
AYE CUZZO!

CHARLES
BOY!

STACY

YO CHEESE!

DEBORAH

PRINCY!

DEBORAH/CHARLES/STACY/GARY
THIS IS YOUR MOMENT!

GARY

AYE CUZZO!

CHARLES

BOY!

STACY

YO CHEESE!

DEBORAH

PRINCY!

DEBORAH/CHARLES/STACY/GARY
THIS IS YOUR MOMENT!

END SONG.

SONG 3: "PRINCE RHYME BOOK ENTRY 1"

CYPHERS
BREATHE, BREATHE, BREATHE, BREATHE.

*(DEBORAH, CHARLES, STACY, LEONARD, JJ
and the CYPHERS slowly fade away as PRINCE
writes in his Rhyme Book. PRINCE makes his
way to his bedroom.)*

PRINCE

(Writing in his Rhyme Book.)

MY FIRST GROWN UP RHYME ENTRY AND IT FEELS UNINSPIRED.

THE GIFTS I RECEIVED LEAVES MORE TO BE DESIRED.

ALL THEY HAD TO DO WAS TAKE A CLOSE LOOK,

AND THEY WOULD DISCOVER ALL I WANTED WAS A NOTEBOOK.

ALL I NEEDED WAS A HOT TRACK, A VERSE AND A DOPE HOOK

TO MAKE HEADS TURN WHEN I PASS, LIKE A NO-LOOK.

READY TO DRIVE NO MORE RIDING SHOTGUN.

EIGHTEEN, I'M A MAN, IT'S TIME I GET TREATED LIKE ONE.

CYPHERS

BREATHE, BREATHE, BREATHE, BREATHE.

END SONG.

<u>SCENE 2:</u> (PRINCE'S BEDROOM/DEBORAH &
CHARLES'S HOUSE.)

THE MC
THIS IS WHERE THE MAGIC BEGINS
PRINCE'S ROOM: WHERE HIS FRIENDS ARE THE
PAD AND THE PEN.
STARING AT AN AD AT A RAPPER GOIN' IN,
ON THE INTERNET, BIG TREY AT IT AGAIN!

*(Lights up on BIG TREY and his GOONS live on
social media. PRINCE looks at his phone. GARY
studies PRINCE'S Rhyme Book.)*

BIG TREY
Yo it's ya boy Big Trey aka C-Town's Finest. I'ma be at Mo
iLLA Saturdays tonight performing my new single. Pull up
and bring ya goons out. We keepin' it all the way gully
tonight!

(BIG TREY'S GOONS react, hyping him up.)

PRINCE
Man, Big Trey needs a hug.

GARY
Yo Cuzzo I know you won that little talent show in sixth
grade but I ain't know you had bars like this.

PRINCE
Just expressing my thoughts.

GARY
It's like poetry! Who knew?

PRINCE

Never judge a book by it's cover!

GARY

This might be on Big Trey's level.

PRINCE

Big Trey's okay...if you like that sort of thing.

GARY

Whatever. Trey got Clifftown on smash.

PRINCE

He just doesn't make my kind of music.

GARY

If he ain't making your kind of music, why don't you sign up for Mo iLLA Saturdays?

(GARY takes out his cellphone.)

PRINCE

Maybe I will!

GARY

Good, it's done.

PRINCE

Wait, what's done?

GARY

We're going to Mo' iLLA Saturdays tonight.

PRINCE

What?

GARY

Just texted my homegirl, Slim. It's her event. She's the new head of A&R at Worldwide Records.

PRINCE
(To himself)

My birthday wish...

GARY

There's a cypher after Big Trey's performance you can get down with.

PRINCE

Holy crap!

GARY

It's time to come out of the hip hop closet and show the world what you can do.

PRINCE

I'm not ready.

GARY

You better get ready. It's like grandpa would say: no guts, no glory!

GARY/PRINCE

Go tell your story.

(Lights up on DEBORAH and CHARLES.)

DEBORAH

Prince Pharaoh Harper! Get down here!

PRINCE

Be down in two seconds!

GARY

I gotta go get fresh. Be back in a few to scoop you.

PRINCE

What do I wear?

GARY

You know how they say "just be yourself"?

PRINCE

Yeah.

GARY

Be the opposite of that. Mo iLLA Saturday's is brutal.

(PRINCE picks up his phone and begins to text.)

PRINCE

Better get my friends there for support.

GARY

Yo, this ain't dance class. Don't embarrass me.

PRINCE

No pressure.

GARY

Just give 'em these dope lyrics and that melanated magic, and they'll love you.

(GARY exits. PRINCE freezes.)

SONG 4: " MAGIC"

PRINCE
STANDING ON THE OUTSIDE
HOPING I'M INVITED IN.
GAZING WITH MY EYES WIDE
AT THE OTHER KIDS WITH MY SKIN.
I TRIED TO FIT IN AMONGST THAT CROWD.
AND THEY SAID: "TRY AGAIN."
GEEZ, WHERE DO I BEGIN?

WHAT IS IT LIKE TO BE ENOUGH?
WHAT IS IT LIKE TO WALK THIS WORLD
NOT SO HYPER-AWARE?
HOW ARE WE THE SAME, YET SEGREGATED?
I'M OVER HERE, THEY'RE OVER THERE.
IF ONLY I HAD...

THAT MAGIC, MAGIC.
IF ONLY I HAD THAT MAGIC, MAGIC.
IF ONLY I HAD THAT
SWAG IN MY STEP
AND A VOICE THEY EXPECT
THAT COMMANDS SOME RESPECT.
GOSH, I REALLY NEED TO GET
THAT MAGIC.

(Lights up on DEBORAH and CHARLES.)

DEBORAH
Prince! What is he doing up there?

CHARLES
Probably twirling in his tutu.

DEBORAH

Will you stop teasing him?

CHARLES

It's not teasing. Just tough love.

DEBORAH

I wish you'd show some love to this dinner table. Been asking you to fix it for weeks.

CHARLES

I'm getting Prince to help me. Teach him another skill besides dance.

DEBORAH

He's auditioning for the Desmond Ballet Conservatory. Trust me, his dance skills are paying off.

CHARLES

Dance ain't a practical career.

DEBORAH

He can enroll at the college for free, if he needs a backup plan.

CHARLES

A black man ain't got no business leaping around in leotards. At least the type who like women.

DEBORAH

Oh, please! You used to rock a Jheri curl, leather pants and high heeled platforms.

CHARLES

Not fair! That was the eighties!

PRINCE
MY BLACK CARD'S NEVER BEEN REVOKED,
'CAUSE IT WAS NEVER GIVEN OUT.
BUT I'VE GIVEN IN TO CONSISTENT DOUBT.
GREW THICKER SKIN, WENT A DIFFERENT
ROUTE.
BUT DEEP DOWN INSIDE I CAN'T HIDE THE
GRIEF:
LABELED A "SELLOUT", "OREO" - THAT WAS
POPULAR BELIEF.

WHAT IS IT LIKE TO BE EMBRACED?
WHAT IS IT ABOUT THE WAY I SPEAK
THAT TURNS THEM AWAY?
WHY IS "BLACK" SO HARD FOR ME
WHEN IT'S SOMETHING I LIVE EVERYDAY?
GOD, I PRAY FOR...
BLACK...

PRINCE/CYPHERS
MAGIC, MAGIC.

PRINCE
IF ONLY I HAD BLACK...

PRINCE/CYPHERS
MAGIC, MAGIC.

PRINCE
IF ONLY I HAD THAT
HOW YOU DANCE ON THE FLOOR
ON THE TWO AND FOUR
A COMMON RAPPORT OF BLACKNESS IN YOUR
CORE.

PRINCE (CONT)
IT'S THE LEAN IN THEIR WALK,
THE BASS IN THEIR TONE.
THE COOL IN THEIR SWAGGER
THAT I'VE NEVER KNOWN.
THE ARC IN THEIR J,
THE STYLE OF THEIR HAIR,
THE SNEAKERS ON THEIR FEET
THAT I COULDN'T WEAR.

(Lights up on DEBORAH and CHARLES.)

CHARLES
I wish he was into something else.

DEBORAH
Dance is his gift. He's better than my students on campus.
All they seem to care about is vape pens, social media likes
and trap music.

CHARLES
There was a time when hip hop was positive. We had Chuck
D, Big Daddy Kane, Kurtis Blow, Rakim ain't even use no
curse words. Shit!

DEBORAH
Now, it's a bunch of mumbling baby gangstas, bragging
about popping pills and poisoning the black community. I'm
so glad Prince isn't into that mess.

PRINCE
I got it! I can't see it now!

PRINCE

THAT'S WHEN I FOUND HIP HOP!
COULD BE MY BLACK THANG!
I'MA BE SPEAKING THAT COOL SLANG,
CONFIDENCE AND BRAVADO LIKE BRUCE
WAYNE.
INTO WU TANG AND OF COURSE 2-CHAINZ!
RECITING MY POETRY
'FRONT OF AN AUDIENCE TO BE A DOPE EMCEE.
NEVER WAS TOTALLY OPENLY
RAPPIN' FOR OTHERS -
MY SONGS I WROTE FOR ME.
BUT I'MA GET COMPLIMENTS,
FOLLOWED BY CONFIDENCE
MANY ACKNOWLEDGEMENTS
FROM ALL THE KIDS WHO ARE PART OF THIS
BLACK POPULACE.
FINALLY I WILL NOT BE ANONYMOUS!

CYPHERS

AYE!

PRINCE

AND 'CAUSE OF THIS RAPPIN STUFF
I WILL BE BLACK ENOUGH TO ADDED
TO THE BADDEST CLIQUE
WHO GOT THE BLACKEST SKIN
I FINALLY HAVE AN IN: THAT MAGIC!

> *(PRINCE puts on a quirky outfit he thinks is hip hop.)*

I'LL BE CONSIDERED COOL
AND I'D BE RESPECTED,
AND I'LL HAVE THE SWAG,
AND I'LL BE ACCEPTED.

PRINCE (CONT)

AND MY BLACKNESS IS NEVER QUESTIONED.
I'LL BE CONSIDERED COOL
AND I'D BE RESPECTED,
AND I'LL HAVE THE SWAG,
AND I'D BE ACCEPTED.
AND MY BLACKNESS IS NEVER QUESTIONED.

THE HANDSHAKES THEY USE,
THE WAY THAT THEY DRESS.
THE RHYTHM THEY HAVE
THAT I DON'T POSSESS.
THE CONFIDENCE THEY SHOW
THAT WE CAN'T RESIST.
THE LANGUAGE THEY SPEAK
THAT SOMEHOW I MISSED!

PRINCE/CONCERT FANS

BLACK MAGIC, MAGIC.
IF ONLY I HAD BLACK MAGIC, MAGIC.
IF ONLY I HAD THAT.

PRINCE

IT'S HOW THE BROTHAS GREET,
HOW YOU NOD TO THE BEAT,

PRINCE/CONCERT FANS

YOUR RESPECT IN THE STREET!

PRINCE

THAT MAKES A MAN COMPLETE.
BLACK MAGIC.
BLACK MAGIC!

END SONG.

CONCERT FANS	DEBORAH
Prince! Prince! Prince!	Prince! Prince! Prince!
Prince!	Prince!

(The CONCERT FANS fade away as PRINCE snaps back to reality.)

DEBORAH

Prince!

(PRINCE enters.)

PRINCE

Yeah?

DEBORAH

Did you turn eighteen and lose your mind?

PRINCE

Sorry, mother, goddess queen of all queens.

DEBORAH

That's better. Now help your daddy fix the table.

PRINCE

But I'm already so fresh and so clean...clean.

DEBORAH

Speak English.

PRINCE

I've just assembled my ensemble for the night which is quite spiffy...spiffy.

DEBORAH

Where are you going tonight?

PRINCE

Me and Gary...

DEBORAH

Gary and I...

PRINCE

Gary and I are going to the...movies.

DEBORAH

Don't be out acting a fool tonight.

PRINCE

I'm not.

DEBORAH

Don't need you ruining your chances of getting in the Desmond Conservatory.

PRINCE

I'll be fine. The final presentation isn't for a few weeks.

DEBORAH

Can't be too careful. You're the best dancer in the school, the Desmond Conservatory should let you in, no questions asked.

CHARLES

You ask me: it's a scheme.

DEBORAH

Nobody asked you.

PRINCE

Everything's a scheme to you, Pop.

CHARLES

'Cause life's a scheme. Now go in my toolbox, and grab that Allen wrench.

(PRINCE grabs a crescent.)

CHARLES

That ain't a Allen, that's a crescent.

(CHARLES grabs the crescent wrench and shoves in into PRINCE'S chest.)

CHARLES

Now take the wrench and twist.

PRINCE

I don't have time for this. Gary will be here any minute.

CHARLES

That can wait. Now screw it in.

(PRINCE tries to screw it in.)

PRINCE

It's stuck.

CHARLES

Pull up your tutu, and put your back in it.

PRINCE

I got a splinter!

DEBORAH

I'll get the tweezers.

(DEBORAH exits.)

CHARLES
Dammit boy, ya mama ain't always gonna be around to baby you.

PRINCE
Don't start.

CHARLES
You wouldn't last one day in jail.

PRINCE
Good thing I don't plan on going.

CHARLES
I'm try'na get you ready for the real world.

PRINCE
By building a table?

CHARLES
By building a business to pass on to you.

PRINCE
What if I don't want to go into business with you?

CHARLES
BOY YOU BETTER PAY ATTENTION, SIT YO' ASS
DOWN AND LISTEN.
I'M GONNA SET YOU UP RIGHT
WITH THE FAMILY BUSINESS FOR YOUR LIFE.
MARK MY WORD, YOU WON'T GET HIRED.
WHY BEG WHEN YOU'LL GET FIRED?
DON'T MATTER HOW IT COMES ACROSS, YOU
GOTTA BE YOUR OWN BOSS.
THIS IS THE REAL LIFE.

PRINCE
I'm gonna be my own boss.

CHARLES
GOTTA KNOW HOW TO PLAY THE GAME 'CAUSE
IT AIN'T NICE.

PRINCE
I play my own game.

CHARLES
THIS IS THE REAL LIFE.

PRINCE
I'll make my own life.

CHARLES
YOU GOTTA MAN UP, DON'T THINK TWICE.
HOW DO YOU EXPECT TO WIN
IF YOU DON'T KNOW HOW OR WHERE TO
BEGIN?

CHARLES (CONT)

IT'S A COLD WORLD, YOU CAN'T TRUST NO
FRIEND.
IF IT DON'T MAKE DOLLARS IT DON'T MAKE
SENSE.
THIS IS THE REAL LIFE. THE REAL LIFE.

PRINCE

HOLD UP, WAIT A MINUTE:
YOU PLAN MY LIFE, AND I DON'T HAVE NO SAY
IN IT?
I'MA BE MY OWN BOSS, I'LL CREATE A
BUSINESS,
BUT WHAT'S THE POINT OF MAKING DIGITS IF
MY HEART AIN'T IN IT?
I AIN'T WITH IT! I AIN'T INTO FIXING CARS,
TRANSMISSIONS, ENGINES, NO TWISTIN' KNOBS
I WANNA MAKE YOU PROUD AND GRATEFUL.
BUT AM I ABLE TO DO THAT WITHOUT FIXING A
TABLE?

CHARLES

TIME: TIME IS ALL YOU HAVE.
TIME IS RUNNING OUT. DON'T FORGET YOUR
TIME.

(DEBORAH enters.)

PRINCE

OH, TIME: TIME TO CHANGE MY LIFE.
TIME FOR ME TO FLY AND LEAVE THIS ALL
BEHIND.

CHARLES

YOU CAN DIE ON YOUR FEET OR LIVE ON YOUR
KNEES.

DEBORAH
(To CHARLES)
YOU ALWAYS ARGUE, YOU ALWAYS FIGHT.
AND FOR WHAT? TO PROVE YOU'RE RIGHT?
(To PRINCE.)
LISTEN TO ME. ALL I ASK IS YOU LISTEN.
MY BABY BOY, DANCE IS YOUR GIFT.
USE WHAT YOU HAVE AND YOU WILL UPLIFT.
THIS IS THE REAL LIFE, I AM GIVING YOU
WISDOM.

CHARLES/DEBORAH
THIS IS THE REAL LIFE.

CHARLES	**DEBORAH**
GOTTA KNOW HOW TO	KEEP ON DANCING.
PLAY THE GAME	
'CAUSE IT AIN'T NICE.	

CHARLES/DEBORAH/PRINCE
THIS IS THE REAL LIFE.
THE REAL LIFE.

CHARLES
THE REAL LIFE.

END SONG.

(GARY enters.)

GARY
What's shakin' ya'll? You ready to roll, Cuzzo?

PRINCE
Like yesterday.

DEBORAH

Since you got money to go out, you got the forty dollars you owe me?

GARY

You take credit?

DEBORAH

You got credit?

GARY

Touché.

DEBORAH
(To PRINCE.)

Be back by twelve.

CHARLES

I need you up bright and early to help me finish with this table.

PRINCE

Can't wait.

DEBORAH

Have you eaten?

PRINCE

Yes.

DEBORAH

Got your cell phone?

PRINCE

Fully charged.

DEBORAH

Hang on, you got some crust in your eye.

*(DEBORAH licks her thumb and wipes
PRINCE'S eye with it.)*

PRINCE

Mom! Stop! Gross! It's so wet!

DEBORAH

That's just love boy. Stop squirming.

PRINCE
(To GARY.)

Can we please go?

DEBORAH

Stay out the south side! We didn't spend eighteen years
raising you so you can get shot in some club.

CHARLES

Relax baby, Gary's taking him out to get his mack on. 'Bout
damn time!

GARY

True.

DEBORAH

Pull up your pants Gary, nobody wanna see your drawers!

GARY

I wouldn't be too sure about that Auntie!

(PRINCE and GARY start towards the door.)

DEBORAH

Excuse me.

*(PRINCE walks over to DEBORAH and gives
her a kiss on the cheek.)*

DEBORAH

Love you, Princy.

(THE MC and the CYPHERS enter.)

PRINCE/THE MC/CYPHERS

Love you too Mom.

*(THE MC and the CYPHERS blow DEBORAH a
kiss.)*

DEBORAH

And I mean it, stay away from South Clifftown!

PRINCE

I will, Mom.

THE MC/CYPHERS

He will, Mom!

SCENE 3: (CLUB UNDERGROUND.)

    (PRINCE and GARY stand outside. From inside, we hear the muffled sound of a crowd and loud rap music.)

THE MC
OFF THEY GO TO...

THE MC/CYPHERS
SOUTH CLIFFTOWN!

THE MC
INTO THE SLUMS WHERE CRIMINALS...

THE MC/CYPHERS
GET DOWN!

THE MC
POLICE BE CLOCKIN', OUTSIDE THEY WATCHIN' WAITIN' FOR SOMEBODY TO PULL A GUN AND START POPPIN'.

CYPHERS
    (Makes gun sound effect.)
POW!

                        END SONG.

    (Two POLICE OFFICERS drag an aggressive HIP-HOP FAN out of the club and slam him onto the ground. PRINCE nervously fidgets.)

PRINCE
You sure we're safe here?

GARY

Would you put your big boy pants on? We good fam.

PRINCE

Just taking in my surroundings.

GARY

The only danger you need to worry about is the cypher on stage. You ready?

>*(PRINCE takes off his jacket to reveal his wacky outfit.)*

PRINCE

Hell yeah, if music be the food of love... let's play on!

GARY

What?

PRINCE

You gotta catch up on your Shakespeare.

GARY

Keep the jacket zipped. You ain't in your bedroom performing in front of your toys.

PRINCE

You spying on me?

GARY

Huh?

PRINCE

I mean, I'm cool dude.

SONG 6: "MO' ILLA"

GARY
You gotta come hard with it. We gotta get on Big Trey's level.

PRINCE
I know, I know.

GARY
You scared?

PRINCE
Yo.

GARY
Yo?

PRINCE
That's yes and no.

GARY
Remember: "No guts, no glory."

GARY/PRINCE
"Go tell your story."

PRINCE
I'm ready.

GARY
Good, 'cause these cats bring that blaze. There ain't nothing like "Mo Illa Saturday's"!

(The scene transforms to inside the small, dark, gritty venue, equipped with an elevated stage. The CYPHERS as HIP-HOP FANS enter. Dance Break.)

THE MC/HIP-HOP FANS
IT'S MO' ILLA! SATURDAYS, IT'S MO ILLA!
IT'S MO' ILLA! SATURDAYS, IT'S MO ILLA!
IT'S MO' ILLA! SATURDAYS, IT'S MO ILLA!
IT'S MO', MO', MO', MO', IT'S MO'...

(GARY and PRINCE enter and approach a CYPHER as a DOORMAN.)

THE MC AS HOST
ID!

GARY
GOT IT.

(GARY and PRINCE flash their ID's. THE MC as a HOST carrying a clipboard approaches with two CYPHERS as BOUNCERS.)

THE MC AS HOST
YOU ON THE LIST?

(GARY points to his name on the clipboard.)

GARY
BAM! G-MONEY, PLUS ONE!

THE MC AS HOST
GIVE'EM A STAMP.

(A BOUNCER stamps them.)

PRINCE

FUN!

BOUNCER

NOW SPREAD'EM.

> *(The BOUNCERS pat GARY and PRINCE down.)*

BOUNCER

GO GET'EM.

PRINCE

HOLY CRAP, IT'S SO CROWDED!

GARY

YOU'VE NEVER BEEN HERE?

PRINCE

MOM NEVER ALLOWED IT.
THIS IS WHERE THE GREAT RAPPERS GO:
LIL POOKIE, PIMPALICIOUS, YOUNG SLAP-A-HO!

GARY

YO BE COOL, YOU ACTING REAL GOOFY.

PRINCE

SORRY, THIS IS KINDA GROOVY.
I NEED TO FIND MY FRIENDS.

GARY

YOUR BALLET BUDDIES?

PRINCE

BALLET *SQUAD*.

GARY

YO CUZ, IT CAN'T MAKE IT BACK TO YOUR
MOM THAT WE AT...

**GARY/THE MC/STACY/LEONARD/JJ/HIP-HOP
FANS**

MO ILLA!

> *(PRINCE looks around and spots LEONARD,
> JJ, and STACY. They wave to PRINCE. SLIM
> enters and takes center stage.)*

STACY

Young Cheesy!

LEONARD

Prince!

JJ

What up dude?

PRINCE

Hey! You guys made it.

STACY

You know I had to come witness the debacle for myself.

PRINCE

I thought you were playing in traffic tonight.

STACY

There was a traffic jam.

LEONARD

You're gonna kill it!

STACY

Don't miss your entrance for this performance like you did ours.

PRINCE

For the hundreth time, I ripped my tights! I couldn't come onstage in a dance belt.

STACY

Better than leaving me on stage alone.

JJ

Ya'll, that was so last year.

LEONARD

Yeah, drop it like it's hot already.

STACY

This ain't the spot for the dancer type.

PRINCE

Tupac took ballet, and he would've definitely hung out here.

STACY

You comparing yourself to Tupac? More like One-Pac.

(Everyone laughs.)

PRINCE

So I'm half way there... thanks!

(SLIM enters and takes the stage.)

SLIM

WHO'S READY TO GET SLAYED?

CYPHERS

WHAT?

SLIM

ANOTHER SATURDAY, ANOTHER DAY TO GET
PAID.

CYPHERS

WHAT?

SLIM

SOMEONE TO GET SIGNED, SOMEONE TO GET
DISCOVERED,

CYPHERS

BY WORLDWIDE RECORDS!

SLIM

AIN'T NOTHING ABOVE IT.
THE NAME'S SLIM: HEAD OF A&R.
ARTIST AND REPERTOIRE. GET WITH YA GIRL
AND BE A STAR.
COMING TO THE STAGE, OUR FEATURED
ARTIST.
THE REIGNING KING OF CLIFFTOWN, REPPIN'
THE HARDEST!
IT'S BIG TREY!

END SONG.

(BIG TREY enters.)

SONG 7: "I'M THE KING"

BIG TREY	BIG TREY FANS
MAN I'M THE KING!	AHHH.
C-TOWN'S FINEST.	AHHH.
FIVE STAR	AHHH.
GENERAL:	AHHH.
GREET ME AS YA	
HIGHNESS.	
NUMERO UNO, DOG	
I'M THE FLYEST.	
BIG TREY!	

BIG TREY	BIG TREY FANS
CAN'T NOBODY DO	HAIL THE KING, OH!
IT LIKE THIS I'M THE	
KING!	

BIG TREY	BIG TREY FANS
I'M THE KING	HE'S THE KING, OH.

BIG TREY	BIG TREY FANS
I'M THE KING!	HE'S THE KING, OH.
	OH!

BIG TREY

BIG TREY!

BIG TREY FANS

AYE!

BIG TREY

GHETTO SUPERSTAR.
KING OF CLIFFTOWN, WHO WANNA GO BAR
FOR BAR?
STRAIGHT FROM THE GUTTER, WHAT'CHU
EXPECT?
I HELD A TECH BEFORE MY FIRST STEP, BET I'M
A THREAT.
I'M THE KING FOR A REASON, I'M THE ONE
THEY BELIEVE IN.
THE REPRESENTATIVE, NEVER SENSITIVE,
NEVER BEATEN.
I'M THE REASON THAT YA'LL EVEN HEARD OF
THE CITY.
PUT IT ON MY BACK, THEN ON THE MAP,
AND THAT'S WHY I'M THE KING!

BIG TREY	BIG TREY FANS
C-TOWN'S FINEST.	AHHH.
FIVE STAR	AHHH.
GENERAL:	AHHH.
GREET ME AS YA	AHHH.
HIGHNESS.	
NUMERO UNO, DOG	
I'M THE FLYEST.	
BIG TREY! BIG	
TREY!	

BIG TREY

MIDDLE FINGERS UP IN THE SKY,
NOW WAVE'EM FROM SIDE TO SIDE.
IF YA'LL READY TO BLAZE AT MO' ILLA
FRIDAY'S
SOMEBODY SAY "GET HIGH".
C-TOWN'S WHERE I DWELL, IT AIN'T HARD TO
TELL.

BIG TREY (CONT)
YOU CAN ASK AROUND, BOY MY NAME RING
BELLS.

BIG TREY FANS
THE NAME RING BELLS!

BIG TREY
GOT WORK FOR THE STREET.
   (To the POLICE OFFICERS.)
WE LIVE BY THE CODE, WE DON'T FUCK WITH
POLICE!

(The POLICE OFFICERS react in disgust.)

BIG TREY FANS
SAY NO TO 5-0!

BIG TREY
ONE THING YOU BETTER GET CLEAR:
MY WORST DAY IS YOUR BEST YEAR
WHEN IT COME TO THE MIC, I DON'T FUCK
WITH THE HYPE
I INJECT FEAR TO GET RESPECT HERE.
TO MAKE THE CHECK CLEAR, IN THE BEST
GEAR
I'MA TAKE OFF LIKE A JET LEER
WHEN I'M SPITTIN' THE VENOM, AND FLIPPIN
THE RHYTHM
MY LYRICS'LL MAKE EM ALL SHED TEARS.
BIG DAWG, YOU SMALL FRY
AND WHEN I'M PISSED OFF, MY 4-5 TAKE YOUR
LIFE.

BIG TREY (CONT)

AND OF COURSE MY NAME RINGS SOUTH TO
THE NORTHSIDE
I'M RAW GUY!
BETTER ASK AROUND, 'BOUT MY STATUS,
CLOWN.
LOOK ME MY EYES, I'M THE CAPTION NOW!
'CAUSE I'M THE...

BIG TREY	BIG TREY FANS
I'M THE KING!	HE'S THE FINEST,
MAN I'M THE KING!	SHINE LIKE A
MAN I'M THE KING!	DIAMOND RING.
MAN I'M THE KING!	HE'S THE FLYEST
	WITH THE SONGS
	THAT HE SINGS.
	HE'S MO' ILLA, HE'S
	THE BEST ON THE
	SCENE.
	YOU CAN'T WIN,
	HE'S THE KING.

BIG TREY	BIG TREY FANS
Man, I'm the king.	BOW DOWN.
Man, I'm the king.	BOW DOWN.

BIG TREY FANS

YOU BETTER BOW DOWN 'CAUSE HE'S THE
KING.

END SONG.

(The BIG TREY FANS go nuts.)

SLIM

Boy, that was fire! Give it up one more time for Big Trey!

(The BIG TREY FANS scream as BIG TREY exits the stage.)

BIG TREY
(To STACY.)
Stacy, Stacy, Stacy! Didn't know you were rolling through.

STACY

Yo, you shut that down.

BIG TREY

That's 'cause I had my muse in the house.

STACY

Here you go.

BIG TREY

Yo, dead ass. We need to go back to my spot so we can inspire each other.

(He attempts to put his arm around STACY, but she steps away.)

STACY

No thank you. Been there, done that.

BIG TREY

We had a good thing.

STACY

Yo, boundaries... you bein' mad extra right now.

LEONARD

Hello! We are not background for your little hip hop reality show.

STACY

Trey. This is Leonard.

LEONARD

Call me Lenny B!

STACY

And JJ.

JJ

Short for... jiggy jammin, leaving jerks jealous while keepin' joints jumpin!

BIG TREY

Shouldn't you be called JJJJJJ?

JJ

I guess so.

PRINCE

Two J's are enough.

STACY

Last and definitely least: Prince.

PRINCE

Funny.

STACY

He's rockin' tonight.

BIG TREY

Oh word, you spit?

PRINCE
(To TREY)
Oh fah-sheezy my neezy. Yup. Cold chillin'... word.

STACY

They're in the dance company with me.

BIG TREY

Wait, so ya'll be wearing tights and shit?

LEONARD

Umm, yes! With the matching dance belts!

PRINCE

Please stop.

SLIM

Y'all know I'm always on the hunt for the newest, rawest, up and coming talent to join the Worldwide Records family, so if that's you... it's time for the...

SLIM/CROWD

BLESS THE MIC CYPHER!

> *(The HIP-HOP FANS form a circle, excited. A RAPPER steps in the middle.)*

SONG 8: "INTERLUDE - THE FREESTYLE CYPHER"

RAPPER

FIX YA FACE HATERS!
YA'LL SEE THE CHAIN HANG GLACIERS,
BLAZIN' MAIN STAGES,
WHILE PAID WITH RAISED WAGES.
GOT PURPLE LIKE LA LAKERS
GLOCK HITTIN' YOU LIKE JOHN WITHERSPOON:
BANG BANG HATERS!
A TRUE HUSTLER: I FALL DOWN AND BOUNCE
BACK.
STAY SHARP LIKE I'M SINGIN' OFF KEY - LAY IT
DOWN FLAT
ANYTHING I SAY I MEANT IT
RAPPERS TALK SLICK SHIT 'TIL I EXERCISE MY
SECOND AMENDMENT.
AND THEY AIN'T SAID NOTHIN' SINCE
WANNA TALK CLOUT, YOU GET TOSSED OUT
LIKE JAZZ IN FRESH PRINCE.
UP IN SOUTH CLIFFTOWN WITH ALL THAT FAKE
JEWELRY.
YA'LL NIGGAS GETTIN' NO BREAD, YA'LL
NIGGAS GLUTEN FREE!

(HIP-HOP FANS react.)

GARY

Get it in Cuzzo!

JJ

Go get em, Prince!

LEONARD

Yeah, sing out Louise.

STACY

Let's see what you workin' with.

(PRINCE steps in and pulls out his Rhyme Book.)

SLIM

You're rapping from your notepad?

PRINCE

Book of rhymes! All the legendary rappers have one.

GARY

Just go already.

PRINCE

THE DIABOLICAL, WITH THE LOGICAL
MANIFESTATIONS.
BREAK 'EM DOWN TO MOLECULES WHEN I
FOLLOW THROUGH EVERY CREATION
BASICALLY I'M AN ODD MIXTURE: I'M LIKE
GODZILLA, BUT MO' ILLA
I'M A MONSTER, BUT BIGGER.
LIKE JACK THE RIPPER, THE SPITTER, CAUSIN' A
RECKLESS MESS
MY RAP IS SICKER, CONSIDER I AM THE NEXT
THE BLESS
WHEN I IMPRESS I GET CHECKS, I'M ON POINT
LIKE INDEX
I INGEST THESE INSECTS, AM I THE KING? THEY
SAY...

PRINCE/HIP-HOP FANS

YES!

(HIP-HOP FANS react to PRINCE, very impressed. BIG TREY approaches him.)

BIG TREY

Oh, you think you're the king?

PRINCE

No, I was just...

BIG TREY

Sound like you wanna battle Big Trey. Yo, keep that beat goin'. This off the dome!

PRINCE

No, wait...

BIG TREY

SAY IT AIN'T SO: I'M BATTLING THE DUDE FROM READING RAINBOW!
IT AIN'T NOTHIN' FOR BIG TREY TO OUT-RAP YOU
SAME WAY IT AIN'T NOTHIN' FOR ME TO OUT-BLACK YOU
YOU AIN'T A THREAT, I CAN TELL BY YOUR LOOK
'CAUSE REALLY, WHAT RAPPER SPITS FROM A NOTEBOOK?
ROLLIN' WITH GEEKS, DOIN' BALLET AND SPINNING?
EXHIBIT A: THIS IS HOW YOU <u>DON'T</u> GET WOMEN.
PRINCE: YOU ARE DELIRIOUS
IT'S A SIGN 'O' THE TIMES, I CAN'T TAKE YOU SERIOUS
LET'S GO CRAZY: TREY SEND SHOTS YA WAY.

BIG TREY (CONT)

BLOODSHED TO YA HEAD, THAT'S A RASPBERRY
BERET.
HOW THE HELL YOU GONE TRY TO COMPETE?
YOU AIN'T A RAPPER - DUDE, YOU ACT WHITER
THAN ME.
PRINCE OVER HERE LIKE "MY GOSH!"
BEAT BY A WHITE GUY, GUESS YOU REALLY
GOT WHITEWASHED.

END SONG.

*(BIG TREY stands nose to nose with PRINCE,
staring menacingly in his eyes. The HIP-HOP
FANS react, whooping, hollering, laughing, etc.)*

SLIM

Yo, those are fighting words!

GARY

Yo, let him have it, Cuzzo!

JJ

Do it man!

*(The Crowd gets more hyped. PRINCE thumbs
through his Rhyme Book.)*

PRINCE

I...I...

BIG TREY

I...I...what?

(PRINCE is silent.)

BIG TREY (CONT)

Thought so. Stick to dance, 'for you get your nuts cracked. And I mean that in the most manly way possible.

(The crowd snickers, then disperses. BIG TREY exits with his crew.)

LEONARD

Wait, that was a Nutcracker joke? Touche mean sir! Touche!

(STACY, LEONARD and JJ console PRINCE.)

JJ

Congratulations.

PRINCE

On what?

JJ

Nothing. It's just something you say after a show.

LEONARD

You gotta get off book.

STACY

That was actually going well, until it wasn't. Keep at it. You're not awful.

(They exit. GARY approaches SLIM.)

GARY

My girl Slim.

SLIM

Your boy is...interesting.

GARY

You serious?

SLIM

I mean, he and his diabolical nerd swag got slaughtered but...

GARY

He's not a battle rapper. He's pen and pad kinda dude... a poet.

SLIM

We already filled our niche category with Deuce Bozo.

GARY

That nut who raps in clown makeup?

SLIM

He's got a following. And poetic bars may work in Clifftown, but Worldwide wants a crossover artist like Big Trey.

GARY

You're head of artist and repertoire. It's your job to show those execs what's up.

SLIM

Execs only want a sad story they can sell to the masses.

GARY

So if I come up with a marketable "story" and....

SLIM

...and produce a hot single...

GARY

Then...

SLIM

Get your followers up...

GARY

You'll sign him...?

SLIM

I'll see what I can do.

GARY

Done. Now what kind of advance we talkin'?

SLIM

Slow your roll. We're not there.

GARY

Just humor me.

SLIM

We've given some up to a hundred G's.

GARY

Word? Prince is signed to my label.

SLIM

You got a label?

GARY

Yeah it's... next level... "Next Level Records". We'll be happy to form a joint venture with you.

SLIM

First get me that hit then we'll talk a deal.

(SLIM exits.)

GARY

My girl, Slim. Bringing in that Worldwide dough. Time for "Next Level" to find some cash flow!

<u>SCENE 4:</u> (DANCE STUDIO.)

(THE MC mysteriously appears with THE CYPHERS.)

THE MC
PRINCE IS IN THE DANCE STUDIO BEFORE CLASS,
JOTTIN' IN HIS RHYME BOOK, WRITING ANOTHER DRAFT.
THINKIN' 'BOUT THE "L" HE TOOK.
HE COULD USE A WIN TODAY 'CAUSE BIG TREY LEFT HIM SHOOK.

<u>SONG 9: "PRINCE RHYME BOOK ENTRY 2"</u>

(PRINCE writes in his Rhyme Book by himself in the dance studio.)

PRINCE
I MUST BE KIDDING MYSELF - THINKING I'M GOOD WITH THE WORDS.
HOW DO I SPEAK ABOUT STRUGGLE IF I LIVE IN THE 'BURBS?
WHERE WAS THE MAGIC WHEN I NEEDED IT?
WHAT'S THE INGREDIENT?
HOW COME WHEN I RAP, NOBODY BELIEVING IT?
EIGHTEEN:

CYPHERS
PLANNING OUT THE REST OF YOUR LIFE.

PRINCE
WHO AM I?

CYPHERS
A KID TRY'NA RAP ON THE MIC.
TRAPPED IN BETWEEN TWO WORLDS OF
AUTHENTICITY.

PRINCE
WONDERING: SHOULD I HAVE DONE IT ALL
DIFFERENTLY?
DID I RUIN MY CHANCES UNWITTINGLY?
I GUESS THAT REMAINS A MYSTERY...

CYPHERS
STANDING ON THE EDGE, YOU HAVE TO JUMP!

END SONG.

*(The bell rings. Lights up on PRINCE.
LEONARD, JJ, STACY and the DANCE
STUDENTS enter in their tights and begin
stretching.)*

JJ
Prince, you're way too nice to be a rapper, dude.

STACY
Yeah, white people love you. That ain't good.

(DANCE TEACHER enters.)

DANCE TEACHER
Alright everyone, listen up! It's that time of year again.
You'll present original dancing duets for your final
presentations. They will be critiqued by the heads of
Desmond Conservatory's dance program and seniors will be
considered for admission into their professional company.

DANCE. TEACHER (CONT)
(The class is excited.)
There are only two slots.

STACY
Two slots?

JJ
Wow. That's it?

LEONARD
Which really means just one because Prince is a shoo-in!

STACY
Shit that sucks.

DANCE TEACHER
Language.

STACY
Damn that sucks.

DANCE TEACHER
Yes it does. So I'd find a partner who will help you raise the bar... pun intended! Now, everyone take your positions! And...

SONG 10: "TOGETHER"

DANCE TEACHER
ONE AND TWO AND THREE AND FOUR.
FOR YOUR FINAL PROJECTS YOU WILL NEED A HIGH SCORE.
ONE AND TWO AND THREE AND FOUR.
THINK ABOUT YOUR PARTNERS, YOU WILL EXPLORE

DANCE TEACHER (CONT)
TOGETHER, JOINED AS ONE.
BEAUTIFUL LINES, STORIES ENTWINED.
HARMONY, ONE ACCORD.
NO IF, AND'S OR BUT'S OR ELSE YOU'RE CUT.

STACY

Cut?

DANCE TEACHER

Cut!

DANCERS
CAN'T BE TOO BIG, CAN'T BE TOO SMALL,
THIS IS THE TEST, ONCE AND FOR ALL.
THIS WILL DETERMINE OUR LIVES.
THE COMPANY PICKS THE ONES WHO PREVAIL.
AND IF I'M NOT PICKED, I'M SURE TO FAIL.
I GOTTA BE AWESOME, TOTALLY AWESOME.
NO SERIOUSLY, TOTALLY AWESOME.
THE DESMOND CONSERVATORY IS LEGIT.
AND IF I'M NOT PICKED THEN I MAY AS WELL
QUIT!

STACY

This is intense.

(Dance break. The DANCE STUDENTS do their best moves as they seek out a partner. PRINCE and STACY are left together. Both are reluctant.)

STACY
HOW THE HELL WE END UP TOGETHER AGAIN?

PRINCE
(To himself)
IT'S PUNISHMENT. AM I BEING CONDEMNED?
(To STACY.)
PLEASE, DON'T BE ANNOYING! AND DON'T
PROVOKE!

STACY
AS LONG AS YOU DON'T CHOKE!

PRINCE
HEY!

STACY
JUST SAYIN...

PRINCE
WHATEVER!

STACY
WHATEVER...

PRINCE
(Sarcastic.)
THIS IS OFF TO A GREAT START!

STACY
JUST MAKE SURE YOU MAKE IT ONSTAGE.

PRINCE
JUST MAKE SURE YOU DO YOUR PART.

STACY
TOGETHER,

PRINCE
JOINED AS ONE.

PRINCE/STACY
BEAUTIFUL LINES, STORIES ENTWINED.
HARMONY, ONE ACCORD.

STACY
NO IF, AND'S OR BUT'S...

PRINCE
OR ELSE...

PRINCE/STACY
WE'RE CUT.

PRINCE/STACY/DANCERS
TOGETHER JOINED AS ONE.

END SONG

SCENE 5: (DEBORAH & CHARLES'S HOUSE.)

THE MC
PRINCE AND STACY NOW PARTNERS A SECOND
TIME AROUND.
THE QUESTION IS: WILL COMMON GROUND BE
FOUND?
MEANWHILE, GARY HAS HIS OWN VISION
FOR HIM AND PRINCE TO TAKE OUT THE
COMPETITION.

(Lights up on DEBORAH, CHARLES, PRINCE
and GARY. GARY is dressed in a new shiny suit.)

DEBORAH
Who's Easter suit did you steal?

GARY
You got jokes.

DEBORAH
And where's my forty dollars?

GARY
Bam! Keep the change.

(Hands her a hundred dollar bill.)

DEBORAH
Wow. A hundred dollar bill?

CHARLES
You a big time mogul now?

GARY
Let's just say, I'm officially a boss.

DEBORAH

We don't need another rap mogul.

GARY

Whatchu' got against rap Auntie?

PRINCE

Let me get the soap box.

DEBORAH

Back in the day, rap was clean, conscious and commercial. Now it's pop pills so you can kill your brother, and rape your sister.

PRINCE

Not all rap is like that.

DEBORAH

Please. Most of it is glorifying drugs, misogyny and guns, doing exactly what they want us to do: destroy each other. Now sit down and eat before I have to kill you.

GARY

You sounding real elderly right now, Auntie. You ready to roll, Cuzzo?

DEBORAH

Where are you going?

PRINCE

I gotta meet Stacy.

CHARLES

You got a date?

PRINCE

No, it's rehearsal.

CHARLES

It's time you start dating. Starting to wonder which way you batting.

DEBORAH

Charles!

CHARLES

Busy twirling and tap dancing. When he need to start tapping some ass!

GARY

That's my cue. I'll check ya later Unk. Auntie... deuces!

(GARY and PRINCE exit.)

DEBORAH

Boy bye.

(Lights up on PRINCE and GARY outside the house.)

GARY

At some point you gotta come clean with ya Moms about what you doing.

PRINCE

I know.

GARY

How you expect to be a rapper and you can't even play your own music, in your own house?

PRINCE

I was hoping to ease my way into that convo.

GARY

We ain't got much time. Worldwide Records wants to sign you.

PRINCE

What? Really?

GARY

Yes sir. I'm working out a venture deal through my label.

PRINCE

Since when do you have a record label?

GARY

Since today.

PRINCE

And where'd you get the money?

GARY

Borrowed it from my baby moms, then Next Level Records was born.

(Lights up on DEBORAH and CHARLES.)

CHARLES

Things are starting to look up baby. Found the perfect space for "Harper and Son".

DEBORAH

Please don't start.

CHARLES

You gonna be singing a different tune once you see what I got up my sleeve.

GARY/CHARLES

I got big plans...

PRINCE

Really?

DEBORAH

Like what?

CHARLES

First we'll celebrate...

DEBORAH

Okay...

CHARLES

Some wine.

DEBORAH

Good.

CHARLES

Some lobster.

DEBORAH

Better...

CHARLES

And then Pop-ster!

(They kiss.)

DEBORAH

Jackpot!

CHARLES

Me and Prince will be raking in the bucks before you know it.

DEBORAH

Not if he makes it into the Desmond Conservatory.

CHARLES

We need to build the Harper legacy. These white boys been passing down their businesses for generations.

DEBORAH

Why don't you ever consult me for help?

CHARLES

You worry too much. My plan will work. We just need to make some sacrifices.

DEBORAH

Sacrifices?

CHARLES

Liquidate assets: furniture, one of the cars, some of your antique jewelry.

DEBORAH

I'm not selling my jewelry.

CHARLES

It's worth a lot of money.

DEBORAH

This is why I can't get involved with this. Talk to me when you have a solid plan. And leave Prince of it.

CHARLES.

Stop sheltering him.

DEBORAH

I'm being a mother! Since when is that a crime?

GARY

You need...

CHARLES

He needs...

GARY/CHARLES

...to quit dance.

GARY

We gotta get your followers up and develop your image.

PRINCE

Develop my image?

GARY	**CHARLES**
Dance is holding you back.	Dance is holding him back.

PRINCE	**DEBORAH**
Says who?	Says who?

GARY	**CHARLES**
Me.	Me.

GARY

We gotta change your story.

PRINCE

How?

SONG 11: "ALL I KNOW"

GARY
WE GOTTA THUG YOU OUT.

PRINCE
NO.

GARY
YOU GOTTA BE MORE REAL. GOTTA BE
GANGSTA,
OR ELSE WE AIN'T GETTIN' THIS DEAL. IT'S
PART OF THE GAME.

PRINCE
WHAT GAME?

GARY
THE RECORD BIZ.
YOU GOTTA BE A DIFFERENT VERSION OF YOU,
THAT'S WHAT IT IS.

PRINCE
I DON'T WANT A DEAL IF I CAN'T BE MYSELF.
NO AMOUNT OF WEALTH CAN BUY YOUR
DIGNITY OR MENTAL HEALTH.
I DON'T UNDERSTAND WHY I SHOULDN'T
DANCE.

GARY

THERE'S A CHANCE FOR A HUNDRED
THOUSAND DOLLAR ADVANCE.

PRINCE

What?

GARY

That's why we need to create the new you.

CHARLES

ALL I KNOW IS YOU FORCED HIM TO FOLLOW
YOUR COURSE.

DEBORAH

Dance is his gift!

CHARLES

ALL I KNOW IS HE'LL BE WORTHLESS IN THE
WORKFORCE.

DEBORAH

He'll be fine!

CHARLES

ALL I KNOW IS THE SECRET YOU HIDE WITH NO
REMORSE!

DEBORAH

We're not discussing that!

CHARLES

THERE IS ONE FACT YOU REFUSE TO ADDRESS.

DEBORAH

WHAT?

CHARLES

YOU NAMED HIM PRINCE, BUT YOU RAISED A
PRINCESS.

DEBORAH

Just finish the table and leave my boy alone.

> *(GARY pulls out a gold chain with the letters
> "GP".)*

GARY

Put this on.

> *(PRINCE puts on the chain.)*

PRINCE

What's the "GP" stand for?

GARY

"Gangsta-P": Your new rap name.

PRINCE

Gangsta-P?

GARY

Prince gotta take a time-out while Gangsta-P takes over.

PRINCE

This is too much. I mean, I wanna make it, but not like this.

GARY

My baby mama lives in South Clifftown. You know that ain't
no place to raise a child. I could care less how we get it, as
long as we get it.

PRINCE

It's actually *"couldn't care less"*.

GARY

Whatever! This is how we gotta do it. It's now or never.

PRINCE

"Now is the winter of our discontent."

GARY

Yeah. Word. Don't you want out of Clifftown? Don't you want more?

PRINCE

I WANT MORE.

GARY

WE NEED MORE. I DON'T KNOW ABOUT YOU, DOG.
BUT I'M TIRED OF LIVING CHECK TO CHECK,
CALLIN' MOM WHEN IT'S TOO HARD. TIRED OF NOT PROVIDING FOR MY BABY GIRL.
HOW DOES A MAN SURVIVE LIVING IN THIS WORLD?
YOU GOTTA PUT YA PRIDE TO THE SIDE
IF YOU WANNA PROVIDE, OTHERWISE YOU WILL BE DENIED.
SO WHAT IF YOU PLAY A ROLE, IT'S ONLY ENTERTAINMENT.
BET YOU WON'T BE COMPLAININ' 'BOUT THAT MILLION DOLLAR PAYMENT!

PRINCE

I HATE IT: THAT IT HAS TO BE THIS WAY:
ROLES WE PORTRAY SO WE CAN RECEIVE SOME PAY.
IMAGES, WE BARTER: GOTTA ACT HARDER INSTEAD OF SMARTER.
DAMMIT, I JUST WANNA BE PRINCE HARPER!
YOU'RE TELLING ME TO BE EVERYTHING THAT I'M NOT
'CAUSE YOU THINK THAT WILL HELP THE MELODIES THAT I DROP.
AND SEE: THESE ARE THE NECESSITIES OF HIP-HOP,
BUT I'M MISSING THE INTEGRITY, TELL ME WHEN DOES IT STOP?

CHARLES

ALL OF MY WORKING LIFE I'VE ASKED MYSELF:
"WHAT IS IT ALL FOR?" PRINCE DESERVES MUCH MORE.

DEBORAH

HE'LL HAVE MORE, A BETTER LIFE THAN YOU AND I.
BUT HE CAN'T LET OPPORTUNITIES PASS HIM BY.

PRINCE/GARY/DEBORAH/CHARLES

ALL I KNOW IS...

PRINCE

I GOTTA GET RESPECT IN CLIFFTOWN.

PRINCE/GARY/DEBORAH/CHARLES

ALL I KNOW IS...

GARY

YOU GOTTA HAVE THE GUTS IF YOU WANT THE
CROWN.

PRINCE/GARY/DEBORAH/CHARLES

ALL I KNOW IS...

CHARLES

WE'LL HAVE A LEGACY!

DEBORAH

HE CAN'T LET US DOWN.

GARY

AIN'T NOTHIN' THEY CAN TELL US,
BUT IF WE DO IT, WE GOTTA DO IT SO THEY
WON'T FORGET US.

PRINCE/GARY/DEBORAH/CHARLES

THAT'S ALL I KNOW.

(CYPHERS enter.)

GARY

CUZZO, NO GUTS, NO GLORY.
DEAR LORD, WE GOTTA CHANGE OUR STORY.
MAY OUR VOICE RING LOUD IF WE'RE
RECORDING.
TIME TO STAND UP, LET GO SO WE CAN FLY
FREE!

| **GARY/PRINCE** | **DEBORAH** |
| NO GUTS, NO GLORY. | KEEP ON DANCIN' |

GARY/PRINCE	**CHARLES**
DEAR LORD, WE GOTTA CHANGE OUR STORY.	A LEGACY...

GARY/PRINCE
MAY OUR VOICE RING LOUD IF WE'RE
RECORDING.
MAY YOUR VOICE RING LOUD!

GARY/DEBORAH/CHARLES/CYPHERS
ALL I KNOW IS...

GARY
IF YOU PLAY THE ROLE WE'LL WIN FOR SURE!

GARY/PRINCE/DEBORAH/CHARLES/CYPHERS
ALL I KNOW IS...

DEBORAH
THERE ARE OBSTACLES HE WILL ENDURE!

GARY/PRINCE/DEBORAH/CHARLES/CYPHERS
ALL I KNOW IS...

CHARLES
HE'S ALL GROWN UP AND HAS TO BE MATURE!

PRINCE
AIN'T NOTHIN' THEY CAN'T TELL US.

PRINCE/GARY/DEBORAH/CHARLES/CYPHERS
BUT IF WE DO IT, WE GOTTA DO IT SO THEY
WON'T FORGET US.

CHARLES
MAKE THE NEIGHBORS...

CHARLES/CYPHERS
JEALOUS!

GARY
LADIES...

GARY/CYPHERS
OVERZEALOUS!

DEBORAH
MY BABY'S SO...

DEBORAH/CYPHERS
PRECIOUS!

PRINCE/GARY/DEBORAH/CHARLES/CYPHERS
THAT'S ALL I KNOW!

> *(PRINCE, GARY, DEBORAH and CHARLES exit.)*

CYPHERS
ALL I KNOW.
ALL I KNOW.

> *(Lights up on STACY in the dance studio.)*

STACY
ALL I KNOW IS THIS COMPANY'S WHERE I WANNA BE.
ALL I KNOW IS I GOTTA GET THAT SPOT, IT'S MY ONLY SHOT.

STACY/CYPHERS
THAT'S ALL I KNOW.

                                        END SONG.

SCENE 6: (DANCE STUDIO.)

> *(STACY stretches. PRINCE enters writing in his*
> *Rhyme Book with his headphones on followed by*
> *THE MC and CYPHERS beatboxing. PRINCE*
> *practices his flow.)*

STACY

Practicing your bars, One-Pac?

> *(PRINCE tucks his Rhyme Book away. THE MC*
> *and CYPHERS fade away.)*

PRINCE

Jotting down whatever pops up in my head.

STACY

Let me hear it.

PRINCE

I'm not in the mood to be clowned today.

STACY

Safe space. I promise.

PRINCE

I feel like Charlie Brown, and you're about to move the
football right before I kick it.

STACY

We're partners. I deserve to know what's going on in that
weird mind of yours.

PRINCE

DO YOU BELIEVE IN LOVE AT FIRST SIGHT?
I HAVE SINCE I WAS TEN:
THE DAY WHEN I FIRST WITNESSED THE PAPER
MEET THE PEN.
SEE HOW THEY ENGAGE, EVERY PAGE IS
SOMETHING PRICELESS.
MAKING A CAGE FEEL LIKE A STAGE THROUGH
THESE DEVICES:
LITERARY, POETIC - OFF THE TOP LIKE A
BONNET.
THE TYPE WHO DO HAIKU, LYRIC, LIMERICK OR
SONNET.
WHAT IS A SHEET OF PAPER? MY ONLY GUIDE
AND SAVIOR
YOU'RE THE LOVE OF MY LIFE, THE FRUITS OF
MY LABOR.

(STACY contemplates.)

PRINCE

What? Not "gangsta" enough for you?

STACY

Actually, it's fuckin' dope.

PRINCE

Really?

STACY

I didn't know you loved hip hop so much.

PRINCE

It's in my spirit as much as ballet.

STACY

That's a crazy mix.

PRINCE

Worldwide Records wants to sign me, but there's a catch.

STACY

What? Selling your soul? Sacrificing a parent? A trip to the "secret" island?

PRINCE

Secret island? Nah, they want me to get my followers up.

STACY

Oh. That's what's up.

PRINCE

And take on a "gangsta" persona.

STACY

See now? That's whack.

PRINCE

What about Trey? You were all into his gangsta act.

STACY

That's because it's not an act for him. He's 'bout that life, you're not.

PRINCE

So, you like him?

STACY

Once upon a time. He's actually sweet when he's not being "Big Trey".

PRINCE

'Alas, that love, so gentle in his view should be so tyrannous and rough in proof.

STACY

You took the words right out of my mouth.

PRINCE

Maybe the story will end happily ever after for you two.

STACY

People already see me as "ghetto" around here, having a boyfriend with the same energy won't help.

PRINCE

I'll take being ghetto over being cheesy anyday.

STACY

I'm just teasing when I say that.

PRINCE

There's truth in every joke.

STACY

Facts. It sucks not being able to be your full self without the labels.

PRINCE

That's why I retreat to my Rhyme Book. I can be whoever I wanna be.

STACY

You eventually have to come back to reality. You have to face Worldwide, and I have to face this audition.

PRINCE

Face it on your own terms.

STACY

Easy for you to say.

SONG 12: "OUR OWN WORLD"

STACY

WHAT DO YOU DO WHEN YOU HAVE JUST ONE
CHANCE
TO MAKE AN IMPRESSION, TO MAKE THEM SAY
"YES"?
WHAT DO YOU DO WHEN YOU ONLY HAVE
DANCE?
NO OTHER WAY OUT, NO OPTIONS FOR
SUCCESS?

PRINCE

You always have options.

STACY

I CAN'T AFFORD TO SLIP.
I CAN'T AFFORD TO MESS UP.
A SECOND CHANCE AIN'T GUARANTEED,
I HAVE TO NAIL MY AUDITION.
I CAN'T AFFORD TO FAIL.
I CAN'T AFFORD TO SLIP UP.
I GOTTA MAKE IT OUTTA CLIFFTOWN.
MY DREAM WILL COME TO FRUITION.

PRINCE

Sounds like we gotta create our own world.

STACY

What in the "Blackman in Wonderland" are talking about?

PRINCE

Follow me!
IF WE WANNA MAKE AN IMPRESSION, THEN WE
GOTTA LET GO.
LET IT FLOW AND PUT ON A SHOW.
GOTTA BE STRATEGIC WHEN WE BRING IT,
MAKE OUR OWN WORLD, AND MAKE THEM
BELIEVE IT.
A LITTLE PAS DE BOUREE HERE, A LITTLE
THERE,
DIRTY DANCING LIFT, PUT YOU IN THE AIR.

STACY

SLOW DOWN, YOU'RE MOVING TOO FAST!

PRINCE

YO, JUST DO THE MATH.

STACY

WHAT MATH?

PRINCE

YOU PLUS ME: THERE'S NO BETTER EQUATION.
SUBTRACT RESTRAINT, THERE SHOULD BE NO
HESITATION.
MULTIPLY OUR VISION, USE THE IMAGINATION.
DIVIDE OUR TIME AND BE PATIENT.

OUR OWN WORLD, WE CAN TAKE A CHANCE IN
OUR OWN WORLD.
LET GO AND DANCE, NOTHING ELSE MATTERS,
WE CAN BE WHATEVER WE WANNA BE.

PRINCE (CONT)

OUR OWN WORLD, WE CAN TURN THIS PIECE
TO OUR OWN WORLD.
ONCE WE RELEASE, NOTHING ELSE MATTERS,
ALL I ASK IS YOU LET YOURSELF BE FREE.

*(PRINCE does a very impressive dance move.
STACY stares at PRINCE with a blank stare.)*

STACY

HA, HA, HA! IT'S FUNNY, WHEN IT COMES TO
DANCE.
YOU'RE LIKE A YOUNG GENE KELLY, SO
ADVANCED.
PERHAPS WITH RAP, YOU SHOULD TAKE YOUR
OWN ADVICE.
AND IT'S QUITE FUNNY WHEN IT COMES TO
RAP,
YOU ARE YOUR WORST CRITIC
LIMITING YOURSELF IN A TRAP.
YOU DON'T HAVE BE "GANGSTA", YOU CAN BE
NICE.

PRINCE

Nice?

STACY

YOU PLUS ME: NO BETTER COMBINATION.
SUBTRACT YOUR FEAR, MANAGE YOUR
EXPECTATION.
MULTIPLY YOUR CHARM: YOUR POWER OF
PERSUASION.
DIVIDE OUR TIME FOR THIS CREATION.

STACY/CYPHERS

OUR OWN WORLD.

STACY
WE CAN BE FREE IN OUR OWN WORLD.
CAN'T YOU SEE? NO ONE ELSE MATTERS,
PLEASE BELIEVE YOU ARE ENOUGH FOR ME.

PRINCE/STACY
OUR OWN WORLD, WE CAN EXPAND IN OUR
OWN WORLD.
TAKE MY HAND. NO ONE ELSE MATTERS,
JUST YOU AND I, WE CAN BE FREE.

*(PRINCE and STACY drift off into their own
world. THE MC and CYPHERS enter as
DANCERS.)*

PRINCE
WE'LL FLIP THE WORLD ON ITS HEAD.

STACY
WE'LL FLIP THE WORLD ON ITS HEAD.

PRINCE/STACY
WHEN WE HAVE TO FIGHT OUR BATTLES,
WE MUST STAND STRONG, WE CAN'T UNRAVEL.

STACY
IF I FALL...

PRINCE
I'M THERE TO CATCH YOU...

PRINCE/STACY
IN OUR OWN WORLD!

*(Dance Break. PRINCE and STACY discover
new dance moves.)*

PRINCE
WHATEVER WE CHOOSE IS OKAY.

STACY
WHOEVER WE ARE IS CORRECT.

PRINCE/STACY
HOWEVER WE ARE IS RIGHT.

PRINCE
I PROMISE I'M HERE.

STACY
I PROMISE I'M HERE.

PRINCE
I AIN'T GOIN' NOWHERE.

STACY
I AIN'T GOIN'.

PRINCE/STACY
I NEVER FELT THIS WAY BEFORE.
OUR OWN WORLD, WE CAN BE FREE IN OUR
OWN WORLD.

(PRINCE kisses STACY. She pulls away.)

END SONG.

STACY
Yooo...

PRINCE
Sorry.

STACY

Take a cold shower.

PRINCE

Yeah. It's past my curfew anyway! My mom's gonna freak out.

THE MC

IT WAS THAT MOMENT, IT HIT IT HIM AND HE
HAD TO STOP.
SOMETHING ELSE PRINCE LOVES AS MUCH AS
HIP HOP!
UNEXPECTED AND PLEASANTLY UNSCRIPTED.
STACY FELT THE SAME, BUT WAS RATHER
CONFLICTED.

(PRINCE begins to exit.)

STACY

Call me.

(PRINCE smiles, then runs off.)

SONG 13: "HAPPILY EVER AFTER"

STACY

I WAS SIX YEARS OLD WHEN
MY MOTHER DIPPED OUT ON MY DAD.
JUST ME AND HIM WAS ALL WE HAD
TO TRY TO MAKE OUR WAY.

LEARNING HOW TO MAKE DUE:
VIENNA SAUSAGE, RAMON NOODS.
RESENTMENT TURNED TO ATTITUDES
UNTIL I TOOK BALLET.

MY LIFE IS NO FAIRY TALE.
I DON'T HAVE A TRUST FUND,
OR A RICH DAD,
OR A BOYFRIEND WITH LOTS OF DOUGH.

MY LIFE IS NO FAIRY TALE.
I COME FROM FREE LUNCH,
AND NO CAR,
WALKIN' THREE MILES TO THE STUDIO.

I WAS FOURTEEN YEARS OLD
WHEN BOYS WERE INTERESTED IN ME
I'D ENTERTAIN IT JUST TO SEE
BUT I FOCUSED ON DANCE.

LOVE'S A POINTLESS CONCEPT
AND PATRIARCHY IS THE PAST.
PRINCE CHARMING COMES BUT DOESN'T LAST
SO WHY GIVE IT A CHANCE?

MY LIFE IS NO FAIRY TALE.
I DON'T NEED A SWEETHEART,
OR A SIDE-PIECE,
OR A BOYFRIEND TO TALK ABOUT.

MY LIFE IS NO FAIRY TALE.
WHY WOULD I NEED LOVE?
I NEED WORK!
WALKIN' THREE MILES TO MAKE IT OUT.

ONE DAY IN THE NEAR FUTURE
I WILL RELAX, I WILL KICK BACK,
I'M POSITIVE.
SOME DAY IN MY NEAR FUTURE
THEY'LL BE NO STRESS,

IT'LL BE LESS INTENSE
AND I WILL LIVE HAPPILY EVER AFTER.

WHO AM I IS THE QUESTION.
STRESSIN' MY DIRECTION SINCE PRINCE
STEPPED IN.
HE IS A BLESSING FULL OF AFFECTION,
OBJECT OF LOVE, BUT I HAVE MY OBJECTIONS.
I'MA BE A BOSS AT ANY COST,
WHETHER I TAKE IT BY FORCE,
SO OF COURSE I'MA RISE ABOVE.
RACIN' LIKE A HORSE, DIVORCED FROM
INTERCOURSE,
TALKIN' NO SHORTS, NO STOPPIN' MY COURSE,
NOT EVEN LOVE!
LOVE? BOY, I NEVER KNEW THE FEELIN':
A WORLD VOID OF ANY KIND OF CEILING.
PURE JOY, AND DAMN IT'S SO APPEALING,
BUT I AVOID 'CAUSE THEN I'D BE REVEALING
MY OWN WORST ENEMY: MY INNER ME,
SO I PUT UP A WALL TO BLOCK ALL THE
ENERGY.
BUT WHEN I'M WITH PRINCE I ACT
DIFFERENTLY,
MY HEART SKIPS A BEAT INSTANTLY.
I TURN INTO A DIFFERENT "ME": ONE THAT I
LOVE, IN FACT.
I FEEL LIKE MY WORLD'S INTACT.
WHERE BEING BROKE DOESN'T MATTER.
AND MONEY'S NO OBJECT.
NO WORRIES: WHAT A SWEET CONCEPT!
THAT'S WHEN I SNAP BACK TO REALITY
SHIT'S SO SAD TO SEE:
NO PRINCE CHARMING, JUST AGONY

FEELIN' LOST INTO THE WOODS AND IT'S A
TRAGEDY.

ONE DAY IN THE NEAR FUTURE
I WILL RELAX, I WILL KICK BACK,
I'M POSITIVE.

SOME DAY IN MY NEAR FUTURE
THEY'LL BE NO STRESS,
IT'LL BE LESS INTENSE, AND I WILL LIVE...

HAPPILY EVER AFTER. HAPPILY EVER AFTER.
HAPPILY EVER AFTER. HAPPILY EVER AFTER.
HAPPILY EVER AFTER. HAPPILY EVER AFTER.
HAPPILY EVER AFTER. HAPPILY EVER AFTER.

ONE DAY IN THE NEAR FUTURE
I WILL RELAX, I WILL KICK BACK,
I'M POSITIVE.

SOME DAY IN MY NEAR FUTURE
THEY'LL BE NO STRESS,
AND LESS INTENSE
AND I WILL LIVE HAPPILY EVER AFTER.

END SONG.

SCENE 7: (STREETS OF CLIFFTOWN, LATE NIGHT.)

THE MC
MEANWHILE PRINCE IS ON CLOUD NINE!
WHAT A SENSATION, WHAT A TIME TO BE ALIVE.
PAST HIS CURFEW, HE DECIDED TO RUN.
HE'S GOTTA GET HOME...

> *(PRINCE enters in a rush. He wears a hoodie
> and sweatpants with a dance bag on his
> shoulder. Two POLICE OFFICERS enter with
> flashlights. They stop PRINCE.)*

POLICE OFFICER 1
WHOA, SLOW DOWN SON.

END SONG.

POLICE OFFICER 2
You look pretty flustered.

PRINCE
Evening, sir.

POLICE OFFICER 2
It's pretty late. Where ya headed?

PRINCE
Home, sir.

POLICE OFFICER 1
Where's home?

PRINCE
(Points in the direction of his home.)
Not far from here.

POLICE OFFICER 2
Where you running from?

PRINCE
Dance rehearsal.

POLICE OFFICER 1
You one of those breakdancers?

PRINCE
No. Ballet.

(POLICE OFFICERS laugh.)

POLICE OFFICER 2
A ballet dancer? That's a new one.

POLICE OFFICER 1
I need to see your ID Twinkle Toes.

PRINCE
Is something wrong?

POLICE OFFICER 1
You tell us, son.

*(PRINCE begins to unzip his dance bag. Both
POLICE OFFICERS draw their weapons
immediately.)*

POLICE OFFICER 1	POLICE OFFICER 2
Keep your hands where I can see them!	Easy! Hands!

PRINCE

What?

POLICE OFFICER 1

You have any weapons in your bag?

PRINCE
(Shaking, holding his wallet.)
No. I was grabbing my ID.

POLICE OFFICER 1

Mind if we look through the bag?

PRINCE

I do not consent to a search.

POLICE OFFICER 2

He's smart, this one.

POLICE OFFICER 1

You're acting awfully suspicious.

(POLICE OFFICER 2 takes a look at his ID.)

POLICE OFFICER 2

Prince? Ha! Like the singer.

POLICE OFFICER 1
(To POLICE OFFICER 2)
Name like that. No wonder you a dancer. Can you dance like Prince, son?

POLICE OFFICER 2

Only one way to find out. Go 'head and dance for us son.

PRINCE

Dance?

POLICE OFFICER 1

You heard him.

> *(Both POLICE OFFICERS hold their weapons at their side.)*

PRINCE

You're not serious.

POLICE OFFICER 2

We got an alert about a suspicious black male in a hoodie. We need to know if you suspicious or not.

> *(Reluctantly, PRINCE begins a dance combination. He is frightened and angry as he does the steps.)*

POLICE OFFICER 2

Well I'll be damned. He is a dancer.

POLICE OFFICER 2

Alright you can stop.

> *(PRINCE stops.)*

POLICE OFFICER 2

I'm impressed.

POLICE OFFICER 1

Looks like we got the wrong guy after all. You can go now.

> *(POLICE OFFICER 2 hands PRINCE back his
> ID and signals for him to leave. PRINCE grabs
> his dance bag and exits slowly.)*

<u>SCENE 8:</u> (DEBORAH & CHARLES'S HOUSE.)

(DEBORAH sits in the kitchen by herself.
PRINCE enters.)

DEBORAH
Prince! I told you to call if you would be late, I was worried
sick!

PRINCE
I was coming home but I got stopped by...

DEBORAH
Between your father being MIA and you missing curfew, I
don't know who's driving me more crazy.

PRINCE
I was rehearsing.

DEBORAH
Until midnight?

PRINCE
Well yeah, but...

DEBORAH
Were you on the south side with Gary?

PRINCE
No!

DEBORAH
Don't lie to me.

PRINCE
I'm telling the truth.

(CHARLES enters intoxicated.)

CHARLES

What a time to be alive!

DEBORAH

Where have you been?

CHARLES

The dream is happening!

DEBORAH

You could've called!

CHARLES

Sorry baby, the meeting with the landlord ran over.

DEBORAH

You're drunk.

CHARLES

I was celebrating.

DEBORAH

What were you celebrating?

CHARLES

Harper and Son!

PRINCE

I'm not working for you Pop.

CHARLES

The landlord's makin' me put down an extra two month's rent. But once that's done it's a wrap!

(CHARLES exits to the bedroom.)

DEBORAH

And where's this extra two months coming from?

(CHARLES reenters with a jewelry box.)

DEBORAH

No Charles!

CHARLES

We'll be set after this!

DEBORAH

Put my jewelry back.

CHARLES

I got a guy that's gonna give me good money for it.

(CHARLES moves towards the door.)

DEBORAH

At midnight?

CHARLES

Just trust me! I'll get you ten times this when we up and running.

PRINCE

Nobody wants to be a part of your stupid auto shop!

CHARLES

Y'all don't believe in me. I'll prove you both wrong.

(CHARLES starts towards the door. PRINCE pushes CHARLES.)

PRINCE

Put it back!

CHARLES

Look who finally decides to take off his tutu and man up. I been waiting for this day.

DEBORAH

Charles, don't...

CHARLES

You wanna be a man? Step up and take your best shot at ya Pops.

DEBORAH

Prince go to your room...

CHARLES

Stay out of this Deborah! Come on big man, gimme your best shot.

> (CHARLES puts the jewelry box down, and sticks out his chin for PRINCE. He pushes PRINCE. PRINCE takes a swing at CHARLES, but CHARLES catches his fist and puts PRINCE in a choke-hold.)

CHARLES

This is how the real world feels.

DEBORAH

Let him go!

PRINCE

I can't breathe...

DEBORAH

Stop it! You're hurting him!

(PRINCE struggles for air.)

CHARLES

If you don't take control, it'll squeeze the life out of you.

DEBORAH

Charles!

CHARLES

And ain't shit you can do it about it but struggle.

DEBORAH

Stop it now before I call the police!

(DEBORAH pushes CHARLES. CHARLES lets PRINCE go. PRINCE gasps for air.)

CHARLES

I was just playin', tryna teach the boy a lesson.

DEBORAH

I want you out of here!

CHARLES

Deborah...

DEBORAH

I said get the hell out of my house!

CHARLES

Babe...

DEBORAH

Now!

(CHARLES exits.)

DEBORAH

Are you okay baby?

(Grabs PRINCE. PRINCE shrugs her off.)

PRINCE

I'm fine.

DEBORAH

Are you sure? You have a bruise on your neck.

PRINCE

I said I'm good.

DEBORAH

Just let me look at it.

PRINCE

Leave me alone.

DEBORAH

Baby...

PRINCE

I'm not a baby. I'm a man, dammit!

SONG 14: "NO GUTS, NO GLORY"

DEBORAH

Oh. You're a man? Okay. Then give me money to pay the
mortgage, lights, and the water bill. How about you move

out and get your own place, *man*? Well? I'm waiting, *man*. I thought so. You wanna cry about being the man, but you don't know a damn thing 'bout acting like one!

(DEBORAH exits.)

PRINCE
WHAT THE HELL IS HAPPENING?
IT'S LIKE ALL AT ONCE, LIFE IS UNRAVELING.
IT'S BAFFLING, THE MOMENT THINGS BECOME CHALLENGING
IS THE MOMENT I START PANICKING, SOMEONE ANSWER ME!

NO GUTS, NO GLORY. DEAR LORD, I GOTTA CHANGE MY STORY.
MAY MY VOICE RING LOUD IF YOU'RE RECORDING.
TIME TO STAND UP, LET GO, AND BE GANGSTA-P.

PERHAPS I WAS WRONG THIS ENTIRE TIME.
THINKIN' I COULD BE MYSELF WHEN I'M WRITING THESE RHYMES.
NOBODY WANNA HEAR MY STORY AS I TELL IT NOW.
THEY'D RATHER GET A GLIMPSE OF A THUG GHETTO-CHILD.
WHAT DO YOU DO WHEN THE WORLD'S TELLIN' YOU
IN ORDER TO SUCCEED YOU GOTTA STRAY FROM WHAT'S TRUE?
THANKS TO POLICE AND WHAT I ENDURED.
WANTED TO BE BLACK ENOUGH, I GUESS I GOT WHAT I WISHED FOR.

(Lights up on GARY.)

GARY

What's good Cuzzo?

PRINCE

I'll do it.

GARY

Do what?

PRINCE

Be Gangsta-P, and this record deal. I ain't playin' no more games.

GARY

That's what I'm talkin' 'bout. Let's get it. No guts, no glory.

GARY/PRINCE

Time to change our story.

(Lights down on GARY.)

PRINCE

WHAT DOES IT MEAN TO BE BLACK?
IS IT BROKEN ENGLISH WE SPEAK? OR THE CLOTHES ON OUR BACK?
IS IT HOW POLICE REACT THINKIN' I GOT A STRAP?
OR IS IT HOW I DANCE BALLET, JAZZ, MODERN AND TAP?
TO COUNTERACT I GOTTA PLAY A CHARACTER: GANGSTA-P.
'CAUSE WHEN YOU DON'T THEY'LL EMBARRASS YA.
SEE, I'MA DO IT WELL. CALL ME DENZEL.

PRINCE (CONT)
OSCAR WORTHY PERFORMANCE, I'M PREPARED
TO PREVAIL.

I'M GONNA JUMP! I'M ON THE EDGE OF THE
CLIFF.
ON THE HIGHEST RIFF, SO HIGH THE CLOUDS I
CAN SNIFF,
ASKING "WHAT IF I TAKE A LEAP?" WILL I HAVE
WINGS TO LIFT?
OR WILL I SINK INTO A DEEP ABYSS?
I'M GONNA JUMP! TIME TO USE MY BLACK
MAGIC:
SOLIDIFY BLACKNESS THROUGH DRASTIC
TACTICS.
NO MORE JOKING, NO MORE LAUGHING,
NO MORE DANCING BALLET, I'MA BLOW UP
RAPPIN'
WHEN I JUMP!

(Lights up on SLIM and GARY.)

GARY
My girl Slim! You ready for this gangsta goodness we 'bout
to bring?

SLIM
Worldwide's signing Big Trey.

GARY
What? You said...

SLIM
My hands are tied.

GARY

I got it: Prince will battle Big Trey for the deal.

SLIM

Battle?

GARY

It'll go viral. Let the people decide.

SLIM

The label just might go for that. But don't let me down G, my career's on the line.

GARY

I got you!

PRINCE

THIS IS FOR MY FREEDOM: FREEDOM FROM MY FAMILY.
FREEDOM TO BE SANE ON THE BRINK OF INSANITY.
I'MA BE COOL, I'MA BE RESPECTED. ACCEPTED.
MY BLACKNESS WILL NEVER BE QUESTIONED.
THIS IS WHAT I GOTTA DO.
BIG TREY: DAMN RIGHT I'M COMING FOR YOU!
IT'S TIME TO GOODBYE TO PRINCE: IT'S BEEN REAL!
(SAY) HELLO TO THE BAD GUY! I'M GETTIN' THAT DEAL!
YEAH! WHAT UP GANGSTA P! I CAN SEE IT NOW!

(We transition to PRINCE'S fantasy. The CYPHERS enter and surround him.)

PRINCE/CYPHERS

NO GUTS, NO GLORY. DEAR LORD, I GOTTA
CHANGE MY STORY.
MAY MY VOICE RING LOUD

PRINCE	**CYPHERS**
IF YOU'RE	I I'M
RECORDING.	
TIME TO STAND UP,	
LET GO, SO I CAN	
FLY FREE.	

PRINCE/CYPHERS

NO GUTS, NO GLORY. DEAR LORD, I GOTTA
CHANGE MY STORY.
MAY MY VOICE RING LOUD

PRINCE	**CYPHERS**
IF YOU'RE	I I'M
RECORDING.	
TIME TO STAND UP,	
LET GO, SO I CAN	
FLY FREE.	

CYPHERS GROUP 1	**CYPHERS GROUP 2**
OOH	AAH
OOH OOH OOH	AAH
OOH	AAH
AAH.	AAH

CYPHERS GROUP 3
AHHHH
AHHHH
AHHHH

DEBORAH
DON'T STOP
DANCING.
KEEP ON DANCING.
DON'T STOP
DANCING.
KEEP ON DANCING.
TURN THIS BOY
INTO A MAN.

CHARLES
ALL MY LIFE I'VE
WORKED TO CLIMB
RAISING PRINCE
THE ENTIRE TIME.
MAKE HIM TOUGH,
DO ALL I CAN.

GARY
ALL I KNOW IS I
WANT MORE.
ALL I KNOW IS I
NEED MORE.

BIG TREY
DOG, I'M THE KING.
MAN, I'M THE KING.
YEAH, I'M THE KING.
YEAH, I'M THE KING.

STACY
MY LIFE IS NO FAIRY
TALE.
CAN I LIVE HAPPILY
EVER AFTER?
 MY LIFE IS NO
FAIRY TALE.
CAN I LIVE HAPPILY
EVER AFTER?

PRINCE
BLACK MAGIC, MAGIC, MAGIC.
BLACK MAGIC, MAGIC, MAGIC!

CYPHERS
LET MY VOICE RING LOUD.

PRINCE
I CAN FLY FREE.

CYPHERS
LET MY VOICE RING LOUD.

PRINCE
I CAN FLY FREE.

CYPHERS
LET MY VOICE RING LOUD.

PRINCE
I CAN FLY FREE.

CYPHERS
I CAN FLY FREE.

(PRINCE stands center stage. Blackout.)

<u>ACT 2</u>

<u>SCENE 1:</u> (VARIOUS LOCATIONS IN CLIFFTOWN/
RECORDING STUDIO.)

> *(THE MC enters with THE CYPHERS wearing
> "gangsta" attire.)*

THE MC
PREVIOUSLY ON "ONCE UPON A RHYME"
PRINCE DECIDES TO TURN TO A LIFE OF CRIME.
HE BECOMES GANGSTA-P FOR WORLDWIDE.
LET'S MEET GANGSTA-P FOR THE FIRST TIME.

<u>SONG 15: INTERLUDE - "PRINCE STUDIO RAP"</u>

> *(Music blasts. PRINCE appears in a recording
> booth, dressed as a futuristic thug rapper. GARY,
> GUERILLA J, MURDER MITCH, two
> CYPHERS as ENTOURAGE and an ENGINEER
> look on.)*

PRINCE
R2 IS RUNNING HIP-HOP.
DIGITAL, DIGITAL ON YOUR LAPTOP.
R2 THUGBOT IN THE BOOTH
HE'S GONNA MAKE YOUR HEAD BOP.

GARY
Thugbot...?!

PRINCE
THE WAY MY LYRICS HIT WITH NO CENSORSHIP
OVER INSTRUMENTS IS SO LIMITLESS.
INFINITE VIVIDNESS FROM INDIGENOUS,

GARY
What?

PRINCE
VILLAINOUS INFAMOUS WICKEDNESS,
YOU SEE ME KILLIN' THIS.
WATCH SON SHINE LIKE PHOTOSYNTHESIS.
AMBIGUOUS IMAGES FOR YOUR SYLLABUS...

END SONG.

GARY
Stop. Indigenous? Photosynthesis? You sound like Bill Nye.
Shit is whack! Come out!

PRINCE
What'd you think of my polysyllabic wordplay? Gangsta,
right?

GARY
No, very ungangsta. What's P2 Tugboat?

PRINCE
R2 Da Thugbot. You said thug it out. I just put my own little
spin on it.

GUERILLA J
Shit's mad corny, son.

MURDER MITCH

Garbage!

PRINCE

Who are you?

GUERILLA J

Guerilla J.

MURDER MITCH

Murder Mitch.

GARY

Your new squad. Gangsta-P needs to be around some real gangstas.

PRINCE

New squad?

GARY

Entourage.

PRINCE

Thanks, but no thanks.

> *(GARY pulls out a blunt. He lights it up and passes it to PRINCE.)*

GARY

Here. It'll help you relax.

> *(PRINCE gives GARY a look.)*

GARY

C'mon, it's legal now.

PRINCE

You know I don't smoke.

GUERILLA J

Hell, I do.
                    (Grabs the blunt. Takes a hit.)
Yo my nigga, this shit right here?

GARY

Yo, save some for the rookie.

> *(GARY grabs the blunt and offers it back to PRINCE.)*

GARY

The fans went wild when Big Trey smoked on stage.

PRINCE

Newsflash: I'm not Big Trey.

GARY

Whatever it takes', right Cuzzo? No guts, no glory.

PRINCE

Fine. Give it here.

> *(PRINCE takes the blunt and takes a hit. He coughs. The ENTOURAGE helps him.)*

PRINCE

See? I feel like an idiot. All this gangsta garbage isn't me.

> *(PRINCE begins to exit.)*

GARY

Worldwide wants to sign Big Trey, not you.

(PRINCE stops.)

PRINCE

You said the deal was done.

GARY

Slim's feelin' you, but her boss wants Big Trey.

PRINCE

Why are we going through all of this then?

GARY

'Cause I told Slim you'd battle Big Trey, and let the people decide. Worldwide might go for it.

PRINCE

I can't beat Big Trey.

GARY

You right. Prince can't beat him. But Gangsta-P can.

SONG 16: "BE COOL, BE GANGSTA"

GARY

AIN'T NOTHIN' TO IT BUT TO DO IT.

ENTOURAGE

UH HUH.

GARY

WHEN I'M FINISHED WITH YOU, YOU GONE BE ROCKIN' OUT THIS MUSIC.

ENTOURAGE

RIGHT.

GARY

FOLLOW MY ADVICE, GRAB SOME PAPER AND A
PENCIL.
A FEW EASY STEPS TO MAKE LIFE A LITTLE
MORE SIMPLE.

**GUERILLA J/MURDER MITCH/ENTOURAGE/
ENGINEER**

STEP ONE:

GARY

NO MORE BALLET.
YOU'LL NEVER BE GANGSTA WEARING TIGHTS
ANY WAY.

PRINCE

I don't wear them in public.

**GUERILLA J/MURDER MITCH/ENTOURAGE/
ENGINEER**

STEP TWO:

GARY

WEAR YOUR HAT LIKE SO:
NOT FRONT, NOT BACK BUT LIKE THIS AND GO!

**GUERILLA J/MURDER MITCH/ENTOURAGE/
ENGINEER**

STEP THREE:

GARY

SAG YOUR JEANS REAL LOW.

PRINCE

IT FEELS REALLY AWKWARD TO LET MY
DRAWERS SHOW.

GARY

TRUST ME, YOU'LL BE THE BADDEST ON THE
SCENE.
AND NEVER LOOK NICE, BOY YOU LOOK MEAN.

*(PRINCE makes an awkward looking mean-mug
face.)*

GARY

NAH MAN, LOOK MEAN! AND NOW YOU GOTTA
WALK WITH THE LEAN.
FOLLOW THESE STEPS, YOU'LL GET YOUR
RESPECT.
OH YEAH, AND BEFORE I FORGET...

*(GARY does a move. PRINCE does his best to
imitate him with no success.)*

GARY

BE COOL.

PRINCE

LIKE THIS?

(PRINCE does an awkward strut.)

**GUERILLA J/MURDER MITCH/ENTOURAGE/
ENGINEER**

BE COOL, BE COOL, BE COOL.

GARY

BE GANGSTA.

PRINCE

How?

116

GARY
INHALE, EXHALE, AND LET IT GO,

GARY	**GUERILLA J/MURDER**
LET IT GO,	**MITCH/ENTOURAGE/**
LET IT GO,	**ENGINEER**
LET IT GO,	GO, GO, GO, GO!
LET IT GO.	

MURDER MITCH
BE GANGSTA: LIKE OJ SIMPSON IN THE CAR
CHASE.

GUERILLA J
GANGSTA: LIKE AL PACINO IN SCARFACE.

GARY
MATTER FACT, HOLD THIS GUN AND PLAY THE
PART.

(GARY pulls out a gun. Hands it to PRINCE.)

PRINCE
GARY, WHERE THE HELL'D YOU GET A GUN?

GARY
WAL-MART. IT'S NOT LOADED. WE JUST GOTTA
MAKE YOU TOUGHER.

MURDER MITCH
SO HOLD IT OUT AND SAY "BREAK YO'SELF
MOTHER...

PRINCE
No!

117

(GARY gives PRINCE the gun.)

PRINCE
WOW, IT'S HEAVY!

GARY
HOLD IT SIDEWAYS, A'IGHT?

PRINCE
I AM LITERALLY A WALKING STEREOTYPE.

GARY
CUZZO: IT'S ALL IN THE IMAGE:
MIMIC THESE GIMMICKS.
YOU CAN'T BE TIMID OR SKITTISH.
HIT 'EM WITH THAT GRIMACE THAT'S VICIOUS.

MURDER MITCH
(Barking.)
LIKE RAHHH!

(PRINCE reacts, scared.)

GARY
REMEMBER CUZ, IT'S STRICTLY BUSINESS.
THEY'LL SAY "GOOD RIDDANCE" IN MINUTES
'CAUSE YOU ARE LIVIN' WITH PRIVILEGE.

PRINCE
AWWW.

GARY
(Hands PRINCE a grill.)
PUT ON THIS GOLD GRILL.

GUERILLA J

YO, THAT'S SO *REAL*"

PRINCE

DO I HAVE TO?

GARY

YES. OR THEY'LL BE NO DEAL.
YOU GOTTA BE TOUGH.

PRINCE

THIS MIGHT BE TOO FAR.

GARY

IT AIN'T FAR ENOUGH.
CAN'T HAVE NOBODY CALLIN' YA BLUFF SO BE
COOL.

GARY

BE COOL.

PRINCE
(Hands GARY back the gun.)
Not with a pistol.

**GUERILLA J/MURDER MITCH ENTOURAGE/
ENGINEER**

BE COOL, BE COOL, BE COOL.

GARY

C'mon,
BE GANGSTA.
Just say it one time...

PRINCE

INHALE, EXHALE, AND LET IT GO,

PRINCE	GUERILLA J/MURDER
LET IT GO,	MITCH/ENTOURAGE/
LET IT GO,	ENGINEER
LET IT GO.	GO, GO, GO, GO!

GARY

Ladies throw this in my bag. Not bad, Cuz, but now you need to let the beast out!

PRINCE

Like Cookie Monster?

MURDER MITCH

Nah, like The Hulk! Now say...

NIGGA I'M A PIMP, NIGGA I'M A PLAYA!
MY NAME IS GANGSTA-P, ILL RHYME SLAYER,
SAY IT!

PRINCE

NEGRO, I'M A PIMP, NEGRO I'M A PLAYA,
MY NAME IS...

MURDER MITCH

Nah fool, I said "nigga". Say "nigga!"

NIGGA I'M A PIMP, NIGGA I'M A PLAYA!
MY NAME IS GANGSTA-P, ILL RHYME SLAYER,
SAY IT!

PRINCE

NINJA, I'M A PIMP, NINJA I'M A PLAYA...

That word doesn't sound right coming outta my mouth!

SONG 17: "SPIRIT OF THE THUG"

GARY
"Nigga" is *our* word. We took that word and flipped it into something good.

MURDER MITCH
That's hip hop!

GUERILLA J
You can't be no gangsta rapper and not say "nigga".

PRINCE
It makes me really uncomfortable.

GARY
What happened to no guts, no glory?

PRINCE
I'm try'na change my story but...

GARY
How did Jay Z, Dr. Dre, and P. Diddy get their power and wealth?

PRINCE
Being gangsta?

GARY
That's right! Being gangsta gave them freedom. You wanna be free, right?

PRINCE
Of course. Freedom is good.

GARY

Correct, and if freedom is good, then gangsta must be good!

PRINCE

Wait, what?

GARY

Would gangstas let their family down?

PRINCE

Maybe.

ALL

No!

PRINCE

No.

GARY

You think a gangsta would let some white boy take your position?

PRINCE

Wow, good point. There really should be like a hip-hop affirmative action program.

ALL

No!

GARY

That's why you gotta be...

PRINCE

Gangsta! I think I got it!

GARY

NO GUTS NO GLORY!

GARY/PRINCE

DEAR LORD WE WANNA CHANGE OUR STORY!
MAY OUR VOICE RING LOUD WHEN WE'RE
RECORDING!

GARY

You feel the spirit?

PRINCE

Of the Lord?

GARY

No fool! I'm talkin' 'bout the spirit of the thug! Man, I need
you to feel it!

PRINCE

I feel somthing.

GARY

That's the spirit.

PRINCE

I think it's the weed.

GARY

Even better.

PRINCE

Wait. Wait. Oh yeah! It's coming! It's coming! I feel it now
my niggaaaaaa!

>   *(The scene transitions into a dark fantasy world*
>   *as the CYPHERS enter as a GANGSTA CHOIR.)*

GARY

YOU KNOW THE SPIRIT OF THE THUG'S IN YOU.

GANGSTA CHOIR

WHOA OH, OH, THE SPIRIT OF THE THUG'S IN YOU.

GARY/GANGSTA CHOIR

IN THE MORNING, IN THE EVENING.
THE SPIRIT OF THE THUG'S IN YOU.

WHEN I WAS A YOUNGIN' AND I WASN'T A THUG.

GANGSTA CHOIR

OOH.

GARY

THE O-G'S HAD SHOW ME A LITTLE TOUGH LOVE.

GANGSTA CHOIR

OOH.

PRINCE

SOMETHING ABOUT THIS JUST DOESN'T SEEM RIGHT.

GANGSTA CHOIR

OOH.

PRINCE

IT FEELS DARK.

GARY

I GOTTA SHOW YOU THE LIGHT. THOU SHALL NOT

GARY/GANGSTA CHOIR

SMILE-ETH.

GARY

THOU SHALL NOT

GARY/GANGSTA CHOIR

SNITCHETH.

PRINCE

I get it!

THOU SHALL NOT

PRINCE/GANGSTA CHOIR

CRY IF YOU GO AND GET SHOT.

PRINCE

THOU SHALL NOT

PRINCE/GANGSTA CHOIR

RUN-ETH.

PRINCE

THOU SHALL NOT

PRINCE/GANGSTA CHOIR

HATETH.

PRINCE/GARY

THOU SHALL NOT

PRINCE/GARY/GANGSTA CHOIR
LET NOBODY TAKE YOUR SPOT.

GANGSTA CHOIR
YEAH!

GARY
THE SPIRIT OF THE THUG'S IN YOU.

GANGSTA CHOIR
WHOA OH OH, THE SPIRIT OF THE THUG'S IN
YOU.

PRINCE/GANGSTA CHOIR
IN THE MORNING, IN THE EVENING.

GANGSTA CHOIR
THE SPIRIT OF THE THUG'S IN YOU.

(PRINCE pulls out the gun.)

PRINCE	**GANGSTA CHOIR**
I'M MO' GANGSTA!	
I'M MO' GANGSTA!	
I'M MO' GANGSTA!	CAN YOU FEEL IT!
I'M MO' GANGSTA!	CAN YOU FEEL IT!
	CAN YOU FEEL IT!
	CAN YOU FEEL IT!

(PRINCE is caught up in the gangsta spirit.)

GANGSTA CHOIR

CAN YOU FEEL IT!
CAN YOU FEEL IT!
CAN YOU FEEL IT!
CAN YOU FEEL IT!

CAN YOU FEEL IT!
CAN YOU FEEL IT!
CAN YOU FEEL IT!
CAN YOU FEEL IT!

CAN YOU FEEL IT!
CAN YOU FEEL IT!
CAN YOU FEEL IT!
CAN YOU FEEL IT!

CAN YOU FEEL IT!
CAN YOU FEEL IT!
CAN YOU FEEL IT!
CAN YOU FEEL IT!

CAN YOU FEEL IT!
CAN YOU FEEL IT!
CAN YOU FEEL IT!
CAN YOU FEEL IT!

GANGSTA CHOIR(CONT'D)

FEEL THE THUG IN YOU!

CAN YOU FEEL THE
THUG IN YOU!

CAN YOU FEEL THE
THUG IN YOU!

CAN YOU FEEL THE
THUG IN YOU!

CAN YOU FEEL THE
THUG IN YOU!

GANGSTA CHOIR(CONT'D)
CAN YOU FEEL! FEEL! FEEL! FEEL! FEEL! FEEL!
THE SPIRIT OF THE THUG IN YOU!

END SONG.

<u>SCENE 2:</u> (DANCE STUDIO/RECORDING STUDIO.)

<u>SONG 17: INTERLUDE - "PRINCE RHYME BOOK ENTRY 3"</u>

> *(Lights up on PRINCE in full "Gangsta-P" mode, along with MURDER MITCH and GUERILLA J. They are in the Recording Studio.)*

THE MC
THE GUNS, THE DRUGS, THE CARS, THE BITCHES,
THE ICE ON HIS NECK, THE THUGS, THE RICHES.
THIS IS GANGSTA-P, DON'T GET IT TWISTED.
PRINCE HARPER'S GONE LIKE HE NEVER EXISTED.

> *(PRINCE raps from his Rhyme Book.)*

PRINCE/MURDER MITCH/GUERILLA J
IT'S ABOUT TO GO DOWN!

> *(Lights up on STACY in the Dance Studio.)*

STACY
(Texting.)
Prince, where the hell are you? Rehearsal started a half hour ago. You better be on your way.

PRINCE/MURDER MITCH/GUERILLA J
IT'S ABOUT TO GO DOWN!

> *(MURDER MITCH and GUERILLA J exit.)*

STACY
(Texting.)
What the hell? You're an hour late. Yo, dead ass - you better be dead or kidnapped. 'Cause I'm starting without you.

PRINCE/MURDER MITCH/GUERILLA J
IT'S ABOUT TO GO DOWN!

STACY
(Texting.)
Yo I'm mad tight right now. My future is riding on this performance. Don't let me down again asshole.

> *(Light down on STACY. Lights up on PRINCE in the recording booth.)*

PRINCE
IT'S ABOUT TO GO DOWN - IF THEY COME FOR GANGSTA-P.
I'M THE REALEST IN THE GAME, IT'S PLAIN TO SEE.
NO MORE MR. NICE-GUY, ROLL WITH A CREW TWICE YA SIZE,
YOU WILL SEE YOUR DEMISE.
YOU BETTER REALIZE - MY LIFE WAS NEVER HEAVENLY.
DON'T BE SURPRISED IF YOU CATCH ME WITH A FELONY.
MAMA STAY STRESSIN' ME, POP MESSED UP THE LEGACY.
GANGSTA-P IS THAT NIGGA, SO DON'T MESS WITH ME!
YEAH!
IT'S ABOUT TO GO DOWN!

END SONG.

*(PRINCE exits the booth and steps outside.
GARY and MURDER MITCH enter from the
other direction as two MASKED THUGS.)*

GARY (AS MASKED THUG)
You Gangsta-P?

PRINCE
Yeah. What up?

MURDER MITCH (AS MASKED THUG)
I heard you supposed to be a real "G".

PRINCE
You damn right.

*(MURDER MITCH as MASKED THUG draws a
gun on PRINCE.)*

MURDER MITCH
You need to run that chain.

PRINCE
I ain't giving you shit. You gotta take it.

MURDER MITCH
Say less.

(GARY reaches for the chain.)

PRINCE
Get off me!

*(PRINCE punches GARY in the eye. GARY
reacts. PRINCE takes off running. MURDER
MITCH shoots PRINCE. He falls to the ground.*

He takes the chain and exits with GARY.
GUERILLA J enters holding a camera phone.
GARY and MURDER MITCH re-enter.)

SONG 19: SONG - "THE TRUTH"

MURDER MITCH
That sounded like the real thing, yo!

> *(PRINCE gets up and checks out the footage on*
> *the camcorder.)*

PRINCE
They're blanks. They're supposed to sound like that!

GARY
You weren't supposed to really hit me.

PRINCE
Sorry, I was in the moment!

MURDER MITCH
You was like Denzel!

PRINCE
Godzilla ain't got nothin' on me!

GARY
It's King Kong fool.

PRINCE
King Kong... Godzilla... I know I felt like a monster. Did you
get the shot?

GUERILLA J
Fasho.

MURDER MITCH

I think we shoulda used real bullets, man.

PRINCE

Then I could really die.

GUERILLA J

Why we doing this again?

PRINCE

To get my followers up. I gotta go viral.

GARY

Otherwise this battle ain't happening.

PRINCE

When Worldwide see's the buzz from this, they'll sign me on the spot.

GARY

You're nobody 'til somebody shoots you.

PRINCE

I'm feelin' like a killer beast right now.

GARY

Once we put this up, there's no turning back.

PRINCE

I'm feelin' like Chewbacca!

(PRINCE growls ala Chewbacca.)

GARY

That ain't gangsta!

MURDER MITCH
REAL THUG FROM THE HEAD TO THE
SHOESTRING.

GUERILLA J
BETTER BOW DOWN NOW THERE'S A NEW
KING.

PRINCE
NIGGAS GOT AT ME, TOOK A SHOT AT ME,
I CAN SEE THEY NOT HAPPY, I'MA SHOW 'EM
HOW WE DO THINGS!

MURDER MITCH/GUERILLA J
G-A-N-G-S-T-A!

PRINCE
NEW KING OF THE STREET, FUCK BIG TREY.
I'M THE HARDEST ARTIST, BETTER BOW DOWN
TO YA SENSAI.

(We see the video uploading.)

MURDER MITCH/GUERILLA J/GARY
HE'S THE TRUTH IN THE BOOTH, YEAH!
GANGSTA-P IS THE TRUTH, YEAH!
HE'S THE TRUTH IN THE BOOTH, YEAH!
GANGSTA, HE'S THE TRUTH!

(Lights up on the HIP-HOP FANS.)

HIP-HOP FAN 1
HAVE YOU HEARD ABOUT THROUGH WORD OF
MOUTH?
NEW YORK TO THE DIRTY SOUTH?
GANGSTA-P WAS HANGIN' WITH HIS G'S,

HIP-HOP FAN 1 (CONT)
AND THEY TRIED TO MURDER AND MURK HIM
OUT.

HIP-HOP FAN 2
SOMEBODY WAS A BIT UPSET...

HIP-HOP FAN 3
CAUGHT ON CAMERA, THE SILHOUETTE.

HIP-HOP FAN 4
THEY TRIED TO SMOKE HIM LIKE A CIGARETTE.

HIP-HOP FANS
NOW IT'S VIRAL ON THE INTERNET.

PRINCE
FIVE THOUSAND!

GUERILLA J
TWENTY THOUSAND!

MURDER MITCH
FIFTY THOUSAND VIEWS GROWING!

HIP-HOP FAN 3
I HEARD HE WAS A DRUG DEALER.
IF YOU MESS WITH HIM, YOU'LL GET YOUR
LEGS BROKEN.

HIP-HOP FAN 4
I HEARD HE WENT TO PRISON. TEN YEARS, IS
WHAT THEY SAID.

HIP-HOP FANS
GANGSTA-P'S THE REAL DEAL, BETTER BE
PREPARED!
HE'S THE TRUTH IN THE BOOTH, YEAH!
GANGSTA-P IS THE TRUTH, YEAH!
HE'S THE TRUTH IN THE BOOTH, YEAH! GANGSTA,
HE'S THE TRUTH!

PRINCE

Got half a million views!

GARY

Still counting!

PRINCE

Yo check out the comments!

GARY

We trending ya'll!

PRINCE

Correction: Gangsta-P is trending, yo!

I AM THE REALEST ALIVE.
NOBODY ELSE CAN GET SHOT AND SURVIVE.
BETTER THAN OTHER RAPPERS WHO ARE
FRAUDS.
WANNABE GANGSTA BUT THEY A FACADE.

PRINCE/GUERILLA J/MURDER MITCH/GARY
OH MY GOD!

PRINCE
WHO ELSE COULD TAKE THESE BULLETS?

MURDER MITCH/GUERILLA J/GARY
AYE!

PRINCE
TELL THESE HATERS COME PULL UP!

MURDER MITCH/GUERILLA J/GARY
AYE!

PRINCE
NEW KING OF CLIFFTOWN, TELL BIG TREY TO
SIT DOWN!

HIP-HOP FANS	**PRINCE/GUERILLA J/ MURDER MITCH/GARY**
HE'S THE TRUTH IN THE BOOTH, YEAH! GANGSTA-P IS THE TRUTH, YEAH! HE'S THE TRUTH IN THE BOOTH, YEAH! GANGSTA, HE'S THE TRUTH!	ONE MILLION! TWO MILLION! FIVE MILLION VIEWS GROWING! TEN MILLION! TWENTY MILLION! THIRTY MILLION, STILL GOING!

GARY
The video got thirty million views!

MURDER MITCH
That joint is viral!

PRINCE
Gangsta-P's alive!

GARY

So "Hip Hop Weekly" wants to shoot a behind the scenes.
Next Level Records is about to blow.

PRINCE

Yo Cuz, you think you should be seen on the show? That
black eye makes you look like a punk.

MURDER MITCH

Yeah, it makes us look mad soft.

GUERILLA J

Like triple-ply toilet paper.

PRINCE

You gotta fall back, yo.

GARY
(To PRINCE.)

What?

PRINCE

We go hard or go home, that's what you said.

GARY

You serious? Yo, I'm the one that booked this!

PRINCE

And now it's time for you to fall behind the scenes.

GARY

This a joke? You wouldn't be shit without me. I made you!

PRINCE

Then go make another me.

(GARY is silent.)

PRINCE (CONT)
That's it. Be cool. Inhale. Exhale.

GARY
Fuck you.

> *(GARY exits. A CYPHER as a
> VIDEOGRAPHER and a BLOGGER enter. The
> BLOGGER interviews PRINCE and snap
> photos. Lights up on BIG TREY and his GOONS
> are reading the magazine article.)*

HIP-HOP FANS GROUP 1	HIP-HOP FANS GROUP 2
HE'S THE KING.	THE NEW KING OF CLIFFTOWN
HE'S THE KING.	TELL BIG TREY TO SIT DOWN!
HE'S THE KING.	THE NEW KING OF CLIFFTOWN
HE'S THE KING.	TELL BIG TREY TO SIT DOWN!
	THE NEW KING OF CLIFFTOWN
	TELL BIG TREY TO SIT DOWN!

BIG TREY
NEW KING OF CLIFFTOWN?
I'MA SHOW THEM HOW I GET DOWN!

> *(They exit. Lights up on SLIM and GARY.)*

SLIM
AYO G, GOOD NEWS, BECAUSE OF ALL THE
YOUTUBE VIEWS:
WORLDWIDE HAS CHANGED ITS MIND.
WE'LL HOST THE BATTLE, WE CAN'T REFUSE.
GANGSTA-P AND BIG TREY GO HEAD TO HEAD,
JUST LIKE YOU SAID. WE CAN'T LOSE...

GARY
YEAH. GREAT NEWS.

*(Lights up on CYPHERS as COLLEGE
STUDENTS in class gathered around a laptop.
DEBORAH enters.)*

DEBORAH
WHAT'S GOING ON?

COLLEGE STUDENT 1
GANGSTA-P!

COLLEGE STUDENT 2
SAID HE WAS SHOT.

COLLEGE STUDENT 3
TOOK IT LIKE A "G".

COLLEGE STUDENT 1
BUT CHECK THIS: HE'S ABOUT TO BATTLE BIG
TREY. LOOK!

*(COLLEGE STUDENT 1 Shows DEBORAH her
laptop.)*

DEBORAH
PRINCE?!

(Lights up on the Dance Studio. LEONARD, JJ STACY and the DANCE STUDENTS go through class.)

STACY
ONE AND TWO AND THREE AND FOUR.
FOCUS WHEN YOU'RE ON THE DANCE FLOOR.
ONE AND TWO AND THREE AND FOUR.
TO GET INTO DESMOND, WE MUST PUSH MORE.

LEONARD
Where's Prince?

(The DANCE STUDENTS look at STACY.)

STACY
Don't look at me, I'm done with him.

(PRINCE enters.)

PRINCE
Who died and left you in charge?

STACY
Where have you been?

PRINCE
Handling business.

STACY
You stood me up.

PRINCE
My bad. I just stopped by to tell y'all, I'm done with dance.

STACY

What?

PRINCE

My career's takin' off. Dance is holding me back.

LEONARD

Are you serious?

JJ

Why are you doing this, Prince?

PRINCE

The name's Gangsta-P now.

JJ

That's just stupid.

LEONARD

And so on the nose.

STACY

You sold out after all.

PRINCE

I'm selling out alright. Check out "Hip Hop Weekly".

STACY

There's more on the line than your fake career. What about our project?

PRINCE

You'll figure it out.

STACY

You're a selfish piece of shit.

PRINCE

And I'm headed straight to the top.

(BIG TREY and his crew enter.)

BIG TREY

If it ain't the gangsta wannabe. Shouldn't you be slipping into your tighty whities?

PRINCE

Shouldn't you be getting ready to get smoked at our battle?

BIG TREY

I'll be ready. What up Stacy? You rollin' with the chump or the champs?

STACY

I don't roll with chumps.

PRINCE

Really?

BIG TREY

That's right. She wants the real thing not a fake.

PRINCE

I got your fake!

BIG TREY

You lookin' at twenty four karat pure gangsta, pat'na.

(BIG TREY lifts his shirt to reveal three bullet wounds on his abdomen.)

BIG TREY

Got the stripes to prove it. Let's see yours Gangsta-P.

PRINCE

I ain't showin' you shit.

BIG TREY

I told you. Don't talk to me 'bout emcees got skills. He's alright...

BIG TREY/BIG TREY CREW

But he's not real!!

>   *(Everyone laughs. PRINCE pulls out a gun and aims it at BIG TREY.)*

PRINCE

Is this real enough for you?

JJ

Oh my God.

LEONARD

Prince...

STACY

What the hell?

>   *(BIG TREY CREW 1 begins to pull out a gun, BIG TREY stops him.)*

BIG TREY

Yeah? Now be a man and pull the trigger.

>   *(Spotlight on PRINCE who is frozen stiff as the gun trembles in his palm. THE MC and CYPHERS surround him. THE MC, unseen by PRINCE, lower's PRINCE'S gun. PRINCE resists and keeps it up.)*

THE MC
LIFE OR DEATH...

CYPHER 1
FREEDOM OR JAIL...

CYPHER 2
HEAVEN OR HELL...

CYPHER 3
WE GOTTA SAVE PRINCE FROM HIMSELF!

THE MC/CYPHERS
BREATHE, BREATHE: INHALE, EXHALE.
THIS IS YOUR LIFE.YOU HAVE A CHOICE.
HOW WILL YOU PROCEED?

> *(PRINCE lowers the gun. A beat. BIG TREY*
> *punches PRINCE in the stomach. PRINCE*
> *collapses to the floor, coughing, as another*
> *GOON films it. BIG TREY points the gun at*
> *PRINCE.)*

STACY
Trey stop!

BIG TREY
Gangsta-P done wrote a check that Prince can't cash. Tell the world you a fraud.

> *(Points to the camera.)*

JJ
Leave him alone.

BIG TREY

Say it.

PRINCE

I am a fraud.

STACY

He gets the point, Trey.

(BIG TREY hands PRINCE his gun back.)

BIG TREY

A little advice: real thugs are try'na get out the hood, not break in. Make sure you take the safety off next time.

(DANCE TEACHER enters PRINCE tucks the gun away.)

DANCE TEACHER

Hey! What's going on here?

BIG TREY

We was just leaving.

(To PRINCE.)

I'll see you at the battle.

HIP-HOP FANS

HE'S THE TRUTH IN THE BOOTH, YEAH! BIG TREY, HE'S THE TRUTH!

END SONG.

<u>SCENE 3:</u> (DEBORAH & CHARLES'S HOUSE.)

> *(Lights up on DEBORAH. She holds a thick*
> *notebook. PRINCE enters.)*

THE MC/CYPHERS
THE TRUTH...

DEBORAH
Thank God! Where have you been?

PRINCE
Makin' moves. I just need to grab some clothes then I'm out.

CYPHERS
THE TRUTH...

DEBORAH
I saw the video.

PRINCE
It was a prank.

DEBORAH
You're jeopardizing your chances of getting into the Desmond Company.

CYPHERS
THE TRUTH...

DEBORAH
Why?

> *(THE CYPHERS start to beatbox.)*

PRINCE
HOW HAVE YOU NOT BEGUN TO SEE?
YOUR OVERLY MOTHERLY WAYS HAVE BEGUN
TO SMOTHER ME
I WANNA BE FREE FROM YOUR CHAINS THAT
BIND ME,
CONFINE AND REMIND ME
THAT I'M LESS OF A MAN, BUT THOSE DAYS
ARE BEHIND ME!

I'm a rapper, Mom.

DEBORAH
What?

PRINCE
I'm done with dance.

CYPHERS
THE TRUTH...

PRINCE
I have a shot at a record deal with Worldwide Records.

DEBORAH
I won't let you to ruin your life.

PRINCE
Just because you weren't good enough to follow your
dreams doesn't give you the right to hold me back from
mine.

(DEBORAH slaps PRINCE.)

PRINCE
I'm leaving.

(PRINCE begins to exit.)

CYPHERS
THE TRUTH.

DEBORAH
Charles isn't your father.

PRINCE
What?

DEBORAH
He's your stepfather.

PRINCE
What are you talking about?

DEBORAH
Your real father died while I was pregnant with you.

PRINCE
Why are you telling me this now?

(The CYPHERS enter. Through movement and dance they reenact the story being told.)

SONG 20: INTERLUDE - "HIP HOP FLASHBACK"

DEBORAH/CYPHERS
THE TRUTH IS HE WAS A RAPPER WITH
CONNECTIONS...

CYPHERS
WITH TWO RIVAL CREWS USING RHYMES AS
THEIR WEAPONS.
BUT THIS WAS AN EXCEPTION:
BEEF SPILLIN' INTO THE STREETS.
WHERE WAS POLICE WHEN THEY NEEDED
PROTECTION?

DEBORAH/CYPHERS
YOUR FATHER WANTED VIOLENCE TO CEASE.

CYPHERS
ORGANIZED A MEETING BETWEEN THE TWO
CREWS SO THEY COULD SPEAK.
HE'D BE THE MEDIATOR THAT WOULD BRING
ABOUT RELIEF
AND CELEBRATE AFTER OVER HIP HOP BEATS.
HE WANTED PEACE.

> *(They raise two fingers making the "peace"
> symbol.)*

CYPHERS
INSTEAD THEY BROUGHT OUT THE PIECE.

> *(Their "peace" symbols turn into a gun.)*

CYPHERS
ONE SHOT INTO THE HEART, HE WAS
DECEASED.

END SONG.

> *(CYPHERS disappear.)*

PRINCE

You've been lying to me all my life?

DEBORAH

I was young and angry. Angry at him.

PRINCE

For what?

DEBORAH

I told him not to go to that battle. He went anyway, and got himself killed. It almost broke me.

PRINCE

You had no right!

DEBORAH

I didn't want you to end up like him! You're a gifted dancer, you don't have to...

PRINCE

Fuck dance. I'm done with dance and I'm done with you.

DEBORAH

Prince wait...

(DEBORAH attempts to stop PRINCE. He recoils at her.)

PRINCE

Don't touch me! You're a terrible mother.

(PRINCE exits.)

DEBORAH

I'M TRYING MY BEST, I DESERVE SOME PRAISE.
I KNOW YOU WILL BE BLESSED SO MANY WAYS.
I'VE MADE MISTAKES BUT AT LEAST I'M
INVOLVED IN YOUR AFFAIRS.
A BOY I'VE ALWAYS KNOWN. BY MY SIDE, YOU
STAYED.
AND NOW THAT BOY IS GROWN, AND FOR THAT
I AM AFRAID.
A BOY NEEDS A MAN WHO TRULY CARES.

BE BETTER, BE WISER, BE STRONGER THAN ME.
BE GREATER, BE HAPPY, LIVE LONGER THAN
ME.
HOLD ON, BE STRONG.
BE SPECIAL, BE SMARTER, MORE CARING THAN
ME.
BE BRILLIANT, BE LOYAL, MORE DARING THAN
ME.
HOLD ON BE STRONG.

THE SOURCE OF MY GRIEF, IT CUTS LIKE A
KNIFE.
I'VE DONE EVERYTHING TO BURY THAT LIFE.
BURY THE SUFFERING, BURY HIS NAME,
BURY THE LIES, BURY THE SHAME.
NO MATTER HOW DEEP YOU BURY THOSE
BONES,
PILE ON THE DIRT, THROW ON THE STONES.
DON'T MATTER WHAT'S WRONG OR RIGHT,
WHAT'S DONE IN THE DARK WILL COME TO
THE LIGHT.

BE BETTER, BE WISER, BE STRONGER THAN ME.

DEBORAH (CONT)
BE GREATER, BE HAPPY, LIVE LONGER THAN
ME.
HOLD ON, BE STRONG.
BE SPECIAL, BE SMARTER, MORE CARING THAN
ME.
BE BRILLIANT, BE LOYAL, MORE DARING THAN
ME.
HOLD ON BE STRONG.

I LOVE YOU, I LOVE YOU, I LOVE YOU.

END SONG.

SCENE 4: (DANCE STUDIO//PRINCE'S BEDROOM/
DEBORAH & CHARLES'S HOUSE.)

> *(Lights up on PRINCE in his room attempting to
> write in his Rhyme Book. Unable to write,
> PRINCE tears out and crumbles page after
> page. He gives up.)*

SONG 22: SONG - "BLANK PAGE"

CYPHER
WHAT DO YOU DO WHEN THERE'S NOWHERE
TO HIDE?
CAN'T FOCUS, FOCUS, FOCUS.
WHAT DO YOU DO WHEN YOU DON'T KNOW
WHY?
FEELING HOPELESS, HOPELESS, HOPELESS.

PRINCE
WHAT IS A SHEET OF PAPER WITH NO WORDS?
NO WORDS?
POURING OUT EMOTIONS THAT DON'T WORK,
DON'T WORK.
WHAT IS A SHEET OF PAPER WITH NO WORDS?
NO WORDS?
STARING AT A BLANK PAGE, A BLANK PAGE.

CYPHERS
STACY.

PRINCE
ALONE.

CYPHERS
MOM.

PRINCE

DESPAIR.

CYPHERS

POP.

PRINCE

NO TRUST.

CYPHERS

FRIENDS.

PRINCE

NOWHERE. WHO AM I? I DON'T CARE.
LIFE IS A NIGHTMARE.
I'VE NEVER BEEN ENOUGH, I'VE ALWAYS
FINISHED LAST.
I'VE NEVER HAD RESPECT, THEY ALWAYS
POINT AND LAUGH.
ALONE IN THIS WORLD, I AM ECLIPSED.
I AM INVISIBLE, I DON'T EXIST.
LAST ON THE LIST. ALWAYS DISMISSED
FEELIN' EMPTY, JUST THE LIFE OF PRINCE.

WHAT IS A SHEET OF PAPER WITH NO WORDS?
NO WORDS?
POURING OUT EMOTIONS THAT DON'T WORK,
DON'T WORK.
WHAT IS A SHEET OF PAPER WITH NO WORDS?
NO WORDS?
STARING AT A BLANK PAGE, A BLANK PAGE.

CYPHERS

FREEDOM.

PRINCE

NO HOPE.

CYPHERS

LIES.

PRINCE

HEARTBREAK.

CYPHERS

DREAMS.

PRINCE

BROKEN.

CYPHERS

LIFE.

PRINCE

HEARTACHE.
NOWHERE TO TURN, WHY AM I HERE?
I'LL NEVER BE FREE, PARALYZED WITH FEAR.
I NEVER TRIED TO JUMP, I'VE ALWAYS HELD MY
TONGUE.
I'VE NEVER LIVED MY LIFE, I ALWAYS CHOSE
TO RUN.
MOM SAYING...

(Lights up on DEBORAH.)

DEBORAH/CYPHERS

"I TOLD YOU SO."

PRINCE

POP SAYING...

(Lights up on CHARLES.)

CHARLES/CYPHERS
"I TOLD YOU SO."

PRINCE
TREY SAYING...

(Lights up on BIG TREY.)

BIG TREY/CYPHERS
"I TOLD YOU SO."

PRINCE	CYPHERS
WHERE TO GO? I	I TOLD YOU SO.
DON'T KNOW, I	WHO AM I
DON'T KNOW.	SUPPOSED TO BE?
I DON'T KNOW.	WHAT AM I
I DON'T KNOW.	SUPPOSED TO DO?
I DON'T KNOW.	WHERE AM I
	SUPPOSED TO GO
WHO AM I?	FROM HERE. HERE.
I DON'T KNOW.	
WHAT TO DO!	WHO AM I
WHERE I GO?	SUPPOSED TO BE?
I DON'T KNOW.	WHAT AM I
I DON'T KNOW.	SUPPOSED TO DO?
	WHERE AM I
	SUPPOSED TO GO
	FROM HERE. HERE.

PRINCE
CAN I FLY FREE LIKE A PAPER IN THE WIND?
JUMP - BE CLOSER TO THE END?
PISTOL IN ONE HAND, PEN IN THE OTHER:

PRINCE (CONT)
FREEDOM FROM BIG TREY, POP, AND MY
MOTHER.
NO WAY TO RECOVER,
I'M ON THE EDGE OF A CLIFF, ON THE HIGHEST
RIFF
SO HIGH THE CLOUDS I CAN SNIFF - ASKING
WHAT IF
I TAKE A LEAP, TAKE A LEAP...
THEN I WILL BE FREE.

PRINCE	**CYPHERS**
I WILL BE FREE.	WHO AM I SUPPOSED TO
I WILL BE FREE.	BE?
I WILL BE FREE.	WHAT AM I SUPPOSED
	TO DO?
	WHERE AM I SUPPOSED
	TO GO
	FROM HERE. HERE.
	WHO AM I SUPPOSED TO
	BE?
	WHAT AM I SUPPOSED
	TO DO?
	WHERE AM I SUPPOSED
	TO GO
	FROM HERE. HERE.
	PRINCE

PRINCE
No more dance. No more rap. I'm done with all of this.

END SONG.

*(PRINCE holds the gun in his hand. DEBORAH
knocks on PRINCE'S door, holding a book.)*

157

DEBORAH

Prince... I know you're upset. I'm leaving this by your door.
It belonged to your father. He said the "Hip Hop Spirits"
would watch over you. I should've trusted him.

(DEBORAH leaves the book at PRINCE'S door,
then exits. PRINCE opens the door. He picks up
the book. A photo falls out. PRINCE picks it up.
Lights up on THE MC.)

THE MC

"ONCE UPON A RHYME NOT LONG AGO,
1973 WAS THE VERY FIRST SHOW.
EMCEEIN', GRAFFITI, DEJAYIN', AND BREAK
DANCE,
REPLACED ABSENT FAMILY MEMBERS AND
GAVE US A CHANCE.
BUT NOW WE RECOGNIZE HIP-HOP'S FIFTH
ELEMENT:
THE KNOWLEDGE,
THE TRUTH, IT'S TIME WE START TELLIN' IT.

THE CYPHERS

IT'S TIME WE START TELLIN' IT.
IT'S TIME WE START TELLIN' IT.

THE MC

THE MC TAKES A STEP OUTTA THE DARKNESS
AND INTO THE LIGHT, FINALLY SEEN BY
PRINCE,
WHO'S OVERWHELMED WITH TRAUMA.
THE MC REVEALS HIMSELF AS HIS BIOLOGICAL
FATHER.

(THE MC steps towards PRINCE. Note: The following underlined phrases are lines from classic rap songs.)

THE MC

Hey young world.

PRINCE
(Startled.)

Wait... dad?

THE MC

He is I and I am him.

PRINCE

What are you doing?

THE MC

Saving you from yourself.

PRINCE

I'm trippin'.

THE MC

Don't pull the thang out unless you plan to bang...

PRINCE

What?

THE MC

You're trying to express yourself, but that don't give you the license to ill.

PRINCE

I don't understand.

THE MC

You gotta be strong for your <u>dear mama</u>. 'Cause <u>it takes two to make a thing go right</u>.

PRINCE

She lied about you.

THE MC

Yeah, sometimes <u>parents just don't understand.</u>

PRINCE

It's ripping me apart.

THE MC

She was trying to <u>protect ya neck</u>. <u>These are the breaks.</u>

PRINCE

I don't need protecting anymore.

THE MC

You're try'na to be a <u>gangsta...gangsta</u>. But <u>you're headed for self-destruction</u>.

PRINCE

It's too late.

THE MC

Then I'll <u>see you at the crossroads</u>.

PRINCE

It's better than here.

THE MC

<u>Keep your head up</u>.

PRINCE

I'm not Gangsta-P. I'm not Prince.

THE MC

Yes, you are. You're a Prince.

PRINCE

No I'm not...

THE MC

When I reminisce over you, my God...your name is royalty.

PRINCE

What?

THE MC

We loved African history. She was the Queen. All hail the Queen!

PRINCE

That sounds right.

THE MC

I was the King of Rock. And you were our little Fresh Prince.

PRINCE

Prince Pharaoh.

THE MC

Yes. The world is yours. Don't follow the leader. Bring the noise!

PRINCE

How?

THE MC

Keep it real.

PRINCE

How?

THE MC

Keep it real.

PRINCE

How?

THE MC

Tell your story. And keep it real.

CYPHERS

KEEP IT REAL. KEEP IT REAL. KEEP IT REAL.

(A loud noise. PRINCE snaps out of his fantasy world.)

PRINCE

Who's there?

(The scene transitions to the living room. CHARLES appears from the darkness. He notices the gun.)

CHARLES

The hell are you doing with a gun?

PRINCE

Get out.

CHARLES

Son, I know you mad...

PRINCE

Don't call me son. You're not even my real father.

CHARLES

She told you?

PRINCE

Y'all been lying to me for eighteen years.

CHARLES

It was the right thing to do at the time.

PRINCE

Right for who? Not me.

CHARLES

We did the best we could.

PRINCE

So did I. But my best was never good enough.

CHARLES

Prince...

PRINCE

Was never man enough, no matter how hard I tried. So how's this? This man enough for you?

> *(PRINCE indicates the gun. A beat. CHARLES pulls out a piece of paper.)*

CHARLES

I don't know how to speak to you young folks. But I hear you rapping in your room at night. Kick a beat.

PRINCE

Say what?

CHARLES

Kick a beat.

PRINCE

You trippin', I ain't kicking no beats!

CHARLES

Come on, just do it. Drop it like it's hot.

(PRINCE beat boxes.)

SONG 23: "POP'S RAP"

CHARLES
I ATTENDED THE SCHOOL OF HARD KNOCKS,
NO COLLEGE DIPLOMAS.
ALL I HAD WAS THESE STREETS, AND THOSE
PROJECT CORNERS.
I WAS HARD HEADED, CAUGHT IN THE SYSTEM,
REFUSED TO LISTEN TO MOTHER GIVING
WISDOM.
MY POP WAS LAZY, NO AMBITION.
CONTENT WITH POVERTY AND HARSH
CONDITIONS.
I KNOW IT'S HARD TO IMAGINE,
BUT FOR ME: FIXING CARS WAS THE BEST
THING THAT HAPPENED.
GAVE ME FOCUS, I LEARNED HOW TO BUILD.
I WAS GOOD AT IT, HIGHLY SKILLED.
I PEEPED THE GAME, THE GENERAL NOTION
AND ONCE I GOT MONEY, MY PLAN WAS IN
MOTION.

CHARLES (CONT)
FELL ON HARD TIMES AND COULDN'T
RECOVER.
THE ONLY PERSON THAT COULD SAVE ME WAS
YOUR MOTHER.
I LOVE HER, SHE'S SO SMART IT'S
INTIMIDATING.
I THOUGHT I COULD IMPRESS HER WITH THE
MONEY I WAS MAKING.
TURNS OUT SHE AIN'T ASK FOR A DIME.
THE ONLY THING SHE EVER ASKED FOR WAS
MY TIME.
SHE TRIED TO MAKE A MAN OF ME.
I WANTED A LEGACY - BUT WHAT'S LEGACY
WITHOUT FAMILY?
YOU'RE A REAL MAN, CAPABLE OF ANYTHING.
YOUR NAME IS PRINCE, 'CAUSE YOU'RE
DESTINED TO BE A KING.

(CHARLES hits his best "rapper" pose.)

END SONG.

PRINCE
That was a'ight. A little old school but a'ight.

CHARLES
Hand me the gun.

(PRINCE hands CHARLES the gun. He puts it in his toolbox.)

CHARLES
How's the dancing going?

PRINCE

Our final dance project's today. I'm not going.

CHARLES

But don't you have a dance partner?

PRINCE

I'm done with dance.

CHARLES

Don't leave that girl hanging. A real man honors his commitment.

PRINCE

Look who's talking. You've been promising to fix the table since forever ago.

CHARLES

You're right. I'm almost done. How 'bout you do the honors and tighten this last leg?

> *(CHARLES hands PRINCE the screwdriver. PRINCE tightens it.)*

CHARLES

Alright let's lift it up, on three: one, two three.

> *(They stand the table up.)*

CHARLES

Looks pretty damn good.

> *(DEBORAH enters.)*

DEBORAH

What are you doing here?

CHARLES

We need to talk.

DEBORAH

About?

CHARLES
(To PRINCE)
Let me talk with your Mom. You go and kill that performance.

(PRINCE exits.)

DEBORAH

You two buddies now?

CHARLES

He's a good kid. Despite what we put him through.

DEBORAH

If you're here to beg don't waste your breath.

CHARLES

I'm not here to beg. Okay I am. Please! I was trippin'. Let me come back.

(The scene shifts to outside the DANCE STUDIO. STACY stretches by herself. PRINCE approaches.)

STACY

So you decided to show up?

PRINCE

Let's just get this over with.

STACY

Don't you have a battle to do?

PRINCE

I dropped out.

(PRINCE begins to put on his gear.)

STACY

You know, I wanted Prince Harper, not Gangsta-P.

PRINCE

And yet, you're running after Trey?

STACY

I'm not running after anybody. You broke my heart.

PRINCE

I guess that makes us even.

STACY

When we danced, you were so...free. It was intoxicating.

PRINCE

That was before I found out my mother lied to me.

STACY

Lied about what?

PRINCE

My father's really my stepdad. And my real father was killed before I was born.

STACY

Damn...

STACY/CHARLES

I'm sorry.

DEBORAH

You thought you'd drop a line, apologize, and pick up where we left off?

CHARLES

I thought we could start over.

DEBORAH/STACY

You let me down.

CHARLES

I can change.

PRINCE

Let me make this right.

STACY

We only rehearsed once. It's impossible.

PRINCE

I remember it.

STACY

It's my future. I'd rather sink on my own ship.

(STACY and DEBORAH begin to walk away.)

DEBORAH

I think we're better off apart.

PRINCE/CHARLES

Wait...

<u>SONG 24: "REWIND"</u>

PRINCE
ONCE UPON A RHYME, YOU AND I REHEARSED.
LEARNED HOW TO TRUST, WE PUT EACH OTHER
FIRST.

STACY
WE'LL FLIP THE WORLD ON ITS HEAD.

PRINCE
WE WILL STAND STRONG.

STACY
THAT'S WHAT YOU SAID.

PRINCE
OUR OWN WORLD, WE CAN BE FREE.

PRINCE/CHARLES
TAKE MY HAND, DANCE WITH ME.

PRINCE
ONE ACCORD, JUST YOU AND I.
CAN WE, CAN WE, CAN WE REWIND?

CHARLES
I'VE MADE MISTAKES, LOOKED DEEP INSIDE.
I'VE HUMBLED MYSELF, SWALLOWED MY
PRIDE.
I'LL SHOW EMOTION, SURRENDER MY HEART.
TREAT YOU LIKE A QUEEN: JUST TELL ME
WHERE TO START.

DEBORAH
REMEMBER? PARTNERS, HUSBAND AND WIFE
'TIL DEATH DO US PART,

CHARLES
MY BEAUTIFUL BRIDE. ONE ACCORD, JUST YOU
AND I
CAN WE, CAN WE, CAN WE REWIND? HOW DID I
BECOME SO BLIND?

CHARLES/PRINCE
CAN WE TURN BACK THE HANDS OF TIME?
CAN WE, CAN WE, CAN WE, CAN WE GO BACK?

DEBORAH
GO BACK.

STACY
GO BACK.

PRINCE
GO BACK.

CHARLES
CAN WE GO BACK?

DEBORAH
GO BACK.

CHARLES/DEBORAH/PRINCE/STACY
CAN WE TURN BACK THE HANDS OF TIME?

DEBORAH
REWIND.

REWIND.

REWIND.

DEBORAH

REWIND.

CHARLES/DEBORAH/PRINCE/STACY/CYPHERS
WHOA YEAH, TURN BACK THE HANDS OF TIME,
YEAH.

> *(Dance Break. PRINCE and STACY perform
> their dance piece to perfection, while
> DEBORAH and CHARLES slow dance in the
> living room.)*

CHARLES/DEBORAH/PRINCE/STACY
TURN BACK THE HANDS OF TIME, YEAH.

DEBORAH/CHARLES
REWIND.

PRINCE/STACY
REWIND.

CHARLES/DEBORAH/PRINCE/STACY/CYPHERS
REWIND?

END SONG.

<u>SCENE 5:</u> (DEBORAH & CHARLES'S HOUSE.)

(Lights up on DEBORAH and POP's house.)

CHARLES

I lost the lease on the space.

DEBORAH

It's not the end in the world.

CHARLES

I'm not worried about it. I just want to put you and Prince first.

DEBORAH

Well how about we build this legacy together?

CHARLES

Like "Harper and Wife"?

DEBORAH

I was thinking "Deborah and Charles".

CHARLES

"Deborah and Charles"? Man, that ain't got no charm!

DEBORAH

You said you're gonna put me first, right?

CHARLES

I'll think about it.

(PRINCE enters. He heads to his room.)

DEBORAH

Prince, I...

PRINCE

You did what you felt was right.

DEBORAH

And...

PRINCE

You're sorry that it turned out like this.

DEBORAH

But...

PRINCE

You need to...

DEBORAH

Boy would you stop cutting me off?
(Rapping.)
I WANTED TO KEEP YOU SAFE, BUT I HAD NO
RIGHT.
IT WASN'T UNTIL TIMES GOT DARK, WHEN I
SAW YOUR LIGHT.
ONE THING A MOTHER MUST KNOW:
WHEN TO LET HER BABY GO. FO-SHO.

I love you, son.

PRINCE

Why everybody think they can rap in this house?

DEBORAH

Don't hate.

(There's a knock on the door. GARY enters.)

CHARLES

What's up man?

GARY

You hiring at your auto-shop?

CHARLES

Why?

GARY

My career's over.

DEBORAH

What did you get yourself into this time?

GARY

I made the deal with Slim to co-sponsor the rap battle. The event sold out in an hour.

CHARLES

That's a good thing, right?

GARY
(To PRINCE.)

Not when the headliner drops out after being exposed as a phony.

CHARLES

Oh.

GARY
(To PRINCE.)

They say you went crying to your momma.

CHARLES

What?

GARY

They even made a hashtag Prince Challenge.

MOM

Prince Challenge?

GARY

It's where kids post themselves posing as thugs while wearing ballet slippers.

CHARLES

Damn, that's disrespectful.

GARY

Internet still undefeated.

PRINCE

I'm gonna battle Big Trey.

GARY

Word?

DEBORAH

What? No.

CHARLES

Baby, let him be grown.

PRINCE

I can't go out like that. I have to.

GARY

And you're cool being seen with me and my black eye?

PRINCE

You did look pretty lame.

GARY

I know.

PRINCE

Let's do this.

DEBORAH

We're coming too. Nobody's hurting my boy!

PRINCE

Mom...

DEBORAH

Man! Nobody's hurting my man.

GARY

All right. No guts, no glory.

(THE MC enters.)

PRINCE/THE MC

Time to change our story.

(PRINCE, GARY, DEBORAH AND CHARLES exit.)

THE MC

AND SO, LADIES AND GENTS: THIS IS WHAT IT COMES TO:
THIS IS THE MIC CHECK - ONE, TWO, ONE, TWO.
HE CLIMBED THE HILL, AND WALKED THE VALLEY.
NOW STAY TUNED FOR THE GRAND FINALE.

(He exits.)

<u>SCENE 6:</u> (CLUB UNDERGROUND.)

<u>SONG 25: "MO' ILLA REPRISE"</u>

> *(SLIM and a RECORD EXEC stand onstage.)*

SLIM
SAME THING DIFFERENT DAY.
THE BATTLE: GANGSTA-P AND BIG TREY.
WORLDWIDE WILL PICK THE SONG WITH
APPEAL.
AND WHOEVER WINS, SIGNS A RECORD DEAL!

> *(STACY, JJ and LEONARD enter.)*

HIP-HOP FANS
IT'S MO' ILLA! SATURDAYS, IT'S MO ILLA!
IT'S MO' ILLA! SATURDAYS, IT'S MO ILLA!

DEBORAH
IT SMELLS IN HERE.

GARY
THAT'S HIP HOP, AUNTIE.

CHARLES
AND BUFFALO WINGS.

DEBORAH
LOOK AT EVERYBODY, THIS PLACE IS PACKED.

GARY
IT'S THE EVENT OF THE YEAR.
NOW IS OUR TIME, WE CAN'T SHOW ANY FEAR.

HIP-HOP FANS
IT'S MO' ILLA SATURDAYS! MO' ILLA!
IT'S MO' ILLA SATURDAYS! MO' ILLA!

(BIG TREY and STACY enter.)

END SONG.

SLIM
Welcome to the battle of the year! A special Mo' Illa
Showcase Fridays! This is the battle for a record deal with
Worldwide Records! Our judges are in the building, it's goin'
down! If you all are ready to battle make some noise! First
up, we got the king himself, Big Trey!

SONG 26: "KEEP IT REAL/JUMP REPRISE"

BIG TREY
This joint is dedicated to the frauds. This is guaranteed to be
your worst nightmare.

KEEP IT REAL: YOU AIN'T NEVER BEEN NO
THUG.
KEEP IT REAL: YOU AIN'T NEVER SOLD NO
DRUGS.
KEEP IT REAL: YOU AIN'T NEVER SHOT NO GUN.
NEVER HAVE, NEVER WILL, YOU AS FAKE AS
THEY COME!

AW, ISN'T THIS CUTE:
LITTLE PRINCESS WANTS TO BATTLE FOR THE
LOOT.
A FAKE GANGSTA POINTIN' A GUN AND NOT
SHOOT.

BIG TRY (CONT)
(HOW'S A) WHITE GUY REMINDING YOU OF
YOUR BLACK ROOTS?
(IT'S) TIME FOR THE BIG REVEAL.
FRONTIN' LIKE SOME THUG,
BUT ACTUALLY A BALLERINA FOR REAL.
IF YOU ASK ME, HE A FRAUD.
'CAUSE NEVER IN MY LIFE I SEEN A GANGSTA
WEARING LEOTARDS.

HIP-HOP FANS
KEEP IT REAL.

BIG TREY
YOU AIN'T NEVER HAD TO HUSTLE.

HIP-HOP FANS
KEEP IT REAL.

BIG TREY
YOU AIN'T NEVER HAD TO STRUGGLE.

HIP-HOP FANS
KEEP IT REAL.

BIG TREY
I'M PUTTIN' THIS PHONY ON BLAST
THE FIRST BLACK GUY I CONSIDER WHITE
TRASH!

HIP-HOP FANS
KEEP IT REAL.

BIG TREY
I'M 'BOUT TO SHOW YA'LL WHO THE KING.

BIG TREY (CONT)

LOOKS LIKE GANGSTA-P'S UNDER SOME
SCRUTINY.
FAKE POSER, I'LL CRUSH YOU CRUCIALLY.
STANKIN' UP THE ROOM, THIS DUDE IS BOOTY
CHEEKS!
DO YOU SEE? HE DON'T KNOW WHO TO BE.
DUDE SWITCH UP LIKE HE GOING THROUGH
PUBERTY.
FIRST IT'S BALLET BUFFOONERY,
NOW IT'S DIFFERENT CLOTHES FROM WHAT HE
WEARS USUALLY,
NOW LOOK AT HIM, ROCKIN' JEWELRY?
HELL NAW DOG YOU AIN'T FOOLIN' ME!
ALL THIS FLIP-FLOPPIN' AIN'T COOL TO ME.
NOW I GOTTA BEAT YOU BRUTALLY, NO
IMMUNITY 'CAUSE YOU CHOOSE TO MOVE SO
STUPIDLY, IT'S LUNACY!
GANGSTA-P IS FAKE, TREY IS A TRUE EMCEE.
THIS AIN'T RAP, THIS IS YOUR EULOGY.
QUIT THE FAKIN' DOG, SPEAK TRUTHFULLY.

HIP-HOP FANS

KEEP IT REAL

BIG TREY

YOU AIN'T NEVER BEEN NO G.

HIP-HOP FANS

KEEP IT REAL.

BIG TREY

YOU REALLY WANNA BE LIKE ME.

HIP-HOP FANS

KEEP IT REAL.

BIG TREY

TIME TO SAY GOODNIGHT TO THIS BITCH
EVERYBODY SAY HELLO TO THE ARTIST
FORMALLY KNOWN AS PRINCE.

HIP-HOP FANS

KEEP IT REAL.

(The Crowd goes wild.)

SLIM

Wow! Big Trey just dropped a bomb! Next up, Gangsta-P!

HIP-HOP FANS

HE'S THE KING, HE'S THE KING. HE'S THE KING,
HE'S THE KING.

> *(HIP-HOP FANS continue to chant. We drift off
> into PRINCE'S inner thoughts and fantasy
> world. Everyone surrounds him.)*

CHARLES

PULL UP YOUR TUTU!

GARY

WOULD YOU PUT YOUR BIG BOY PANTS ON?

BIG TREY

YOU ACT WHITER THAN ME!

STACY

WHITE PEOPLE LOVE YOU. THAT AIN'T GOOD.

MURDER MITCH

GARBAGE!

SLIM

YOU'RE RAPPING FROM YOUR NOTEPAD?

(The CYPHERS begin to strip him of his Gangsta-P outfit.)

BIG TREY

STICK TO DANCE.

GUERILLA J

THAT SHIT'S MAD CORNY SON!

CHARLES

BUSY TWIRLING AND TAP DANCING!

STACY

MORE LIKE ONE PAC.

DEBORAH

MOVE OUT AND GET YOUR OWN PLACE, MAN!

JJ

YOU'RE WAY TOO NICE TO BE A RAPPER.

GARY

YOU GOTTA BE A DIFFERENT VERSION OF YOU.

BIG TREY

PRINCESS!

CYPHERS

KEEP IT REAL. KEEP IT REAL.
KEEP IT REAL. KEEP IT REAL.

(PRINCE thumbs through his Rhyme Book. He is paralyzed.)

PRINCE

MAGIC, MAGIC. IF I ONLY I HAD…

(THE MC approaches him and hands him the mic.)

THE MC

Jump.

CYPHERS

Jump.

PRINCE

Jump! Come on!

> I NEED YOU TO JUMP! IF YOU FEEL THE PRIDE
> AND YOU'RE FEELING ALRIGHT WITH WHO'S
> INSIDE
> JUMP IF I DON'T CARE WHAT A HATER GOTTA
> SAY,
> I AIN'T GOT NO FEAR!
>
> P TO THE R-I-N-C-E
> THE NAME IS PRINCE AND I'M 'BOUT TO BLOW
> EMCEE'S
> STRAIGHT OFF THE MIC, YES I WEAR TIGHTS.
> SIMILAR TO MY RAP STYLE, MAD TIGHT.
> THE WAY MY LYRICS HIT WITH NO CENSORSHIP
> OVER INSTRUMENTS IS LIMITLESS.
> INFINITE VIVIDNESS FROM INDIGENOUS.
> VILLAINOUS INFAMOUS WICKEDNESS, YOU SEE
> ME KILLIN' THIS.
> WATCH THE SON SHINE LIKE PHOTOSYNTHESIS!
> JUMP! 'CAUSE I'LL ALWAYS BE TRUE.
> AND STICK TO MY GUNS WITH WHATEVER I DO!
> JUMP! 'CAUSE I LOVE MYSELF.

PRINCE (CONT)
I DON'T NEED MONEY AND HOES, BITCHES AND
WEALTH.
IT'S TIME TO JUMP!

WHEN I WANNA HAVE FUN,
ME AND MY CREW FLOW, YEAH WE GET THE
JOB DONE.

THE FLOW'S OFF THE HOOK, I'LL LEAVE YOU
SHOOK
GIMME A WORD TO RHYME, I DON'T NEED A
NOTEBOOK!

STACY
AUTHENTIC.

PRINCE
EVERYTHING THAT I EXHIBIT IS NOT A
GIMMICK,
IT'S QUITE TERRIFIC.
EVERY LYRIC AND HIEROGLYPHIC, I'M PUSHIN'
THE LIMIT
PAINTIN' A PICTURE THAT'S VIVID' CAUSE YOU
KNOW I'M AUTHENTIC!

DEBORAH
FREEDOM!

PRINCE
I CALL IT LIKE I SEE 'EM.
IF I WAS BIG TREY, BOY I WOULDN'T WANNA BE
'EM.
I'LL ROCK ANY STADIUM, ANY COLOSSEUM.
WITH OR WITHOUT PER DIEM I'LL STILL FEEL
FREEDOM!

BIG TREY

OREO.

PRINCE

TREY CALLED ME "OREO".
WHAT AN ORIGINAL JOKE. COOL STORY BRO.
GO 'HEAD AND RAP WITH YOUR BORING FLOW.
I'D RATHER DANCE TO CHOREO WITH MY
POINTED TOE.

WHAT MAKES ME LESS BLACK?
IS IT BECAUSE I BEHAVE OPPOSITE
OF WHAT YOU EXPECT ME TO ACT?
LIKE A MODERN DAY MINSTREL SHOW,
SPITTIN' FLOWS 'BOUT PIMPS AND HOES
IN STEREOTYPICAL CLOTHES?
REDUCING MY BLACKNESS
TO THE STUPIDEST FASHIONS
'CAUSE YOU'RE ONLY USED TO
SEEING BLACK DUDES IN CASKETS?
IT'S HUMOROUS AND I'M LAUGHING
BUT IT'S REALLY SAD 'CAUSE
YOU ARE TELLING THE TRUTH THROUGH YOUR
ACTIONS

(Addresses the audience.)

PRINCE

I RECOGNIZE THIS HYPOCRITE AMONG US
TAKING OUR HISTORY FROM US,
SHOULD MAKE YOU SICK TO YOUR STOMACHS.
MAINLY BECAUSE IT'S THE INDIGENOUS WHO
SUFFERS.
YOU KNOW WHO YOU SOUND LIKE?

PRINCE/HIP HOP FANS
CHRISTOPHER COLUMBUS!

PRINCE
YOU STEAL SWAG FROM MY SISTAS AND MY
BROTHAS
BUT IF ONE OF US GET SHOT ARE YOU
MARCHING WITH US FOR JUSTICE?
DIDN'T THINK SO. TYPICAL, IN FACT.
BUT TATOOS AND CRIMINAL RECORDS DON'T
MAKE YOU BLACK.
BUT HOW LUCKY YOU ARE YOU CAN
APPROPRIATE
TALK THE SLANG, ROCK THE GEAR AND GO
CREATE.
HOW LUCKY YOU ARE
TO CREATE A BLACK PROFILE
BUT NOT GET PROFILED AT ALL!

YOU CAN MIMIC OUR SWAG AND HAND
GESTURES
BUT YOU'LL NEVER KNOW THE STRUGGLE OF
OUR ANCESTORS.
SO YOU WILL NEVER DISRESPECT US.
IN THIS HOUSE OF HIP HOP, YOU'RE LUCKY
THAT YOU'RE EVEN ON THE GUEST LIST!
QUESTIONING MY BLACKNESS? NICE TRY.
WITH A MISINFORMED CROWD, YEAH THAT
MIGHT FLY
BUT IGNORANCE I WON'T ABIDE BY.
YOU'RE NOT EVEN A GREAT RAPPER, YOU'RE
JUST GOOD FOR A WHITE GUY.

JJ/LEONARD
DANCE!

PRINCE

TAKE A GLANCE, PEEP MY <u>RELEVE</u>, MY TENDU
STANCE.
BALLET VOCABULARY BITCH! FRANCE!
SO ADVANCED IN HIP HOP AND DANCE.

(He performs the dance steps as he raps them.)

PRINCE

STAY IN MY POSITION, MAKE 'EM HOP LIKE A
TEMPS LEVE.
BATTEMENT ANY HATER, OVER THEM I GRAND
JETE.
GIVING ME ATTITUDE, MAN YOU AIN'T HALF AS
RUDE.
SO I'M GONNA ASSEMBLE AT ANY MAGNITUDE.
THERE'S NOTHING LEFT TO PROVE.
SO I'MA WEAR MY TIGHTS AND BUSS OUT MY
BALLET MOVES.

*(PRINCE does an exquisite dance move. The
HIP-HOP FANS love it.)*

PRINCE

YOU SAY I'M NOT BLACK 'CAUSE OF MY
CLASSICAL MOVES?
NEWSFLASH DUDE: BEETHOVEN WAS BLACK
TOO!

HIP-HOP FANS

OOOOOOOOOH!

(The HIP-HOP FANS join in the dance.)

PRINCE/CYPHERS

JUMP!

PRINCE
IF YOU WANNA BE FREE
FROM HATERS WHO TELL YOU WHO YOU
SHOULD BE?

CYPHERS
JUMP!

PRINCE
IF YOU'RE FIGHTING FOR EDUCATION
JUST SO WE CAN BETTER THE NATION.

DEBORAH
That's right!

CYPHERS
JUMP!

PRINCE
IF YOU'RE BUILDING A FACTORY
FOR YOUR FAMILY LEGACY THEN...

CHARLES
That's my boy!

CYPHERS
JUMP!

PRINCE
(To BIG TREY.)
IF THEY THOUGHT THEY COULD KEEP YOU IN A
BOX
UNTIL YOU BROKE ALL THE LOCKS! THEN
JUMP! JUMP!
EVERYBODY JUMP! JUMP! JUMP!
EVERYBODY JUMP! JUMP! JUMP!

(The HIP-HOP FANS reacts.)

PRINCE	**HIP-HOP FANS**
THIS IS MY MOMENT.	JUMP, JUMP,
DO I RUN? OR DO I OWN	EVERYBODY, JUMP,
IT?	JUMP
CAN'T STOP, I GOTTA	JUMP, JUMP...THAT
KEEP GOING.	MAGIC! MAGIC! MAGIC!

PRINCE/HIP-HOP FANS
EVERYBODY JUMP!

END SONG.

(The HIP-HOP FANS goes wild.)

SLIM
Woooow! Dope battle guys! But now it's time to decide.
(Addresses the audience.)
Who won this battle folks? Big Trey?
(The HIP-HOP FANS cheer.)
Or Prince?

(The HIP-HOP FANS goes wild.)

HIP-HOP FANS
Prince! Prince! Prince! Prince! Prince!
Prince! Prince! Prince! Prince! Prince!

SLIM
We're gonna see what our judges think.

(Time stands still. SLIM talks with the RECORD EXEC. SLIM'S smile quickly turns to shock.)

SLIM

We have a winner. Let's hear it for the newest member of
The Worldwide family and a one hundred thousand dollar
advance...

*(He looks at the RECORD EXEC who sternly
indicates "Big Trey".)*

SLIM

Big Trey.

CHARLES

Big Trey?

(The HIP-HOP FANS are confused.)

GARY

Prince won that battle!

JJ	**LEONARD**
He was robbed!	This sucks!
DANCE TEACHER	**DEBORAH**
Come on! Prince won!	No, ya'll cheated my boy!

GARY

Yo Slim!

SLIM

I'm not making the decisions here. I told you before: gangsta
always sells.

GARY

Well do what's right! Let them know what's up!

(The HIP-HOP FANS boo. SLIM exits.)

<u>SCENE 7</u>: (BACKSTAGE OF CLUB UNDERGROUND.)

<u>SONG 27: "THIS IS YOUR MOMENT"</u>

GARY
PRINCE!

CHARLES
PRINCE!

STACY
PRINCE!

DEBORAH
PRINCE!

DEBORAH/CHARLES/STACY/GARY
THIS IS YOUR MOMENT.

GARY
PRINCE!

CHARLES
PRINCE!

STACY
PRINCE!

DEBORAH
PRINCE!

DEBORAH/CHARLES/STACY/GARY
THIS IS YOUR MOMENT.

DEBORAH/CHARLES/STACY/GARY/CYPHERS
AS THE WORLD SPINS, AND THE PAGE TURNS,
A NEW CHAPTER WILL BEGIN.
ONE DOOR SHUTS, ANOTHER OPENS UP
AND TOMORROW RUSHES IN.
WELCOME TO EIGHTEEN.
YOU ARE A GROWN UP.
IT'S JUST BEGINNING. (YOU'RE)
STANDING ON THE EDGE: IT'S TIME TO JUMP!

THE MC
HE LOST THE BATTLE, NOW IT'S BACK TO
SQUARE ONE.
WHAT HAPPENS NOW, WHEN IT'S ALL DONE?
SEARCHING FOR THAT MAGIC - 'CAUSE YOU
GOTS TO HAVE IT
ONLY TO DISCOVER MORE THAN YOU
IMAGINED!

(DEBORAH and CHARLES enter.)

CHARLES
Why the hell would you let me force you into working in an
auto shop?

PRINCE
I didn't.

CHARLES
You have a hip hop career!

PRINCE
That's what I've been try'na tell you.

CHARLES
You made us proud, son.

PRINCE

Thanks Pop.

DEBORAH

They would give the white rapper a deal. Appropriating our art. See, I've been saying this for years...hip-hop is ours!

PRINCE

Really, Mom?

DEBORAH

Don't think because you're a big time rap star, I won't be in the front row at one of your rap recitals.

PRINCE

They're concerts, Mom. Not recitals.

DEBORAH

Whatever. I want tickets.

PRINCE

Yes ma'am.

> *(DEBORAH clears her throat. PRINCE smiles, then gives her a kiss on the cheek.)*

DEBORAH

Proud of you, man.

CYPHERS

IT'S TIME TO JUMP!

> *(LEONARD, JJ, and STACY enter.)*

THE MC
WHAT DO YOU DO WHEN YOU KNOW YOU'RE
WRONG?
PICKING UP THE PIECES AT THE END OF THE
SONG?
PUT YOUR PRIDE ASIDE, 'CAUSE WHEN IT'S ALL
SAID AND DONE
CAN'T FORGET YOUR FRIENDS FROM DAY ONE.

PRINCE
Thanks for coming guys. And I'm sorry for...

STACY
Being a dick?

JJ
Being a jackass?

LEONARD
Damn, you took mine.

STACY
Nice dance moves for a rapper.

PRINCE
Thanks.

(DANCE TEACHER enters.)

DANCE TEACHER
I thought it might round out the night with good news.
Stacy...Leonard.

*(She hands STACY and LEONARD envelopes.
They open them and read. LEONARD smiles.
STACY is taken aback for a moment.)*

STACY
I made it.

DANCE TEACHER
Congratulations.

STACY
Thank you!

(STACY hugs DANCE TEACHER.)

STACY
Wait, what about Prince?

DANCE TEACHER
Prince, you're a gifted dancer. But it is abundantly clear what path you should take.

PRINCE
That's okay with me. Congrats Stacy. You did it!

(They hug.)

CYPHERS
IT'S TIME TO JUMP!

THE MC
WHAT DO YOU DO WHEN YOU HAVE ONE CHANCE
TO MAKE THEM SAY "YES"?
NO OTHER OPTIONS FOR SUCCESS?
TO HELP YOURSELF IS TO HELP OTHERS.
ESPECIALLY RIVALS WHO TURNED TO LOVERS.

STACY
You were awesome out there.

PRINCE

You inspired me.

STACY

I do what I can.

PRINCE

Where do we go from here?

STACY

I really like you, Prince. But it's hard to live in my own world if I'm so wrapped up in everyone else's. Let's be friends for now.

PRINCE.

I guess parting is such sweet sorrow.

(She kisses him on the cheek.)

PRINCE

Take all the time you need. I ain't going nowhere.

STACY

Oh yes you are, you're going to the top.

DEBORAH/CHARLES/GARY/STACY/CYPHERS
BREATHE, BREATHE: INHALE, EXHALE.
YOU ARE EIGHTEEN. YOU ARE A MAN.
NOW IT'S TIME YOU LEAD.
BREATHE, BREATHE: INHALE, EXHALE.
NOW THAT YOU HAVE BECOME A MAN
NOW YOU WILL SUCCEED.

GARY

Yo Cuzzo. You like a lit match floatin' in gasoline.

PRINCE

What?

GARY

You about to blow up. Tell 'em, Slim.

SLIM

You clearly won that competition.

PRINCE

I thought so.

SLIM

I decided it's time for me to do my own thing.

PRINCE

You're leaving Worldwide?

SLIM

I already left. Gary and I are partners now.

GARY

Slim's got the investors on lock! Next Level Records is going to the next level.

PRINCE

Wait, what?

SLIM

No label politics, just good music.

GARY

All we need now is to sign our first artist.

> (*GARY looks at PRINCE. PRINCE looks at DEBORAH.*)

DEBORAH
It's time to jump.

DEBORAH/CHARLES/GARY/STACY/CYPHERS
Prince! Prince! Prince! Prince!

GARY
PRINCE!

CHARLES
PRINCE!

STACY
PRINCE!

DEBORAH
PRINCE!

DEBORAH/CHARLES/STACY/GARY
THIS IS YOUR MOMENT.

GARY
PRINCE!

CHARLES
PRINCE!

STACY
PRINCE!

DEBORAH
PRINCE!

DEBORAH/CHARLES/STACY/GARY
THIS IS YOUR MOMENT.

END SONG.

SONG 28: "YOU ARE ENOUGH (FINALE)"

PRINCE
THAT MAGIC, MAGIC: THE WHOLE TIME I HAD
THAT MAGIC, MAGIC.
THE WHOLE TIME I HAD IT.

THE MC
ONCE UPON A RHYME NOT LONG AGO
CITY OF...

THE MC/CYPHERS
CLIFFTOWN...

THE MC
IS WHERE WE...

THE MC/CYPHERS
END THIS SHOW.

THE MC
THE PRIDE OF ALL HIS...

THE MC/CYPHERS
COMMUNITY!

THE MC
BECAUSE HE SEIZED...

THE MC/CYPHERS
OPPORTUNITY.

THE MC
A RAPPER BY THE NAME OF...

THE MC/CYPHERS
PRINCE HARPER!

THE MC
SINCE A KID HE DANCED IN...

THE MC/CYPHERS
BALLET.

THE MC
AND FINALLY HE ALLOWED...

THE MC/CYPHERS
HIMSELF...

THE MC
TO LIVE LIFE IN...

THE MC/CYPHERS
HIS OWN WAY.

PRINCE
THE SON OF A TEACHER,
THE SON OF A BUSINESSMAN,
AND THE SON OF A RAPPER,
WAY DIFFERENT THAN
ANYTHING YOU'VE EVER SEEN BEFORE
A BALLET DANCING EMCEE SPITTIN' THE RAW!
MANY THOUGHT IT WAS IMPLAUSIBLE
A YOUNG BLACK MALE, SO WELL-ROUNDED...

THE MC

NOT POSSIBLE!

PRINCE

DIDN'T EVEN BELIEVE IT MYSELF.
TRY'NA BE SOMEBODY ELSE...

THE MC

YOU JUST NEEDED HELP.

PRINCE

AND THERE I WAS, WATCHING THEM.
TRYING HARD JUST TO FIT IN.
JUST TO SEE I'M UNIQUE
AND THERE'S NO BOX BUILT FOR ME.
TRY'NA CHANGE WHO I AM
TO BE COOL AND BE A MAN.
TO REALIZE BEING DIFFERENT SET ME FREE.

I AM ENOUGH, ENOUGH.
I AM ENOUGH, ENOUGH.
I AM ENOUGH, ENOUGH.
I AM ENOUGH, ENOUGH.

I USED TO STAND ON THE OUTSIDE
HOPING TO BE INVITED IN.
PUTTING ON A FRONT, THEN THEY'D TELL ME
"GO TRY AGAIN."
WONDERED 'BOUT LIFE - WHAT IF I HAD
LIGHTER SKIN?
TRY'NA FIND PEACE, I HAD TO FIND IT WITHIN.
NOW FOR THE FIRST TIME I DISCOVERED MY
MAGIC.
I DON'T GIVE A DAMN AND IT FEELS
FANTASTIC!

PRINCE (CONT)
I CAN FINALLY BE UNAPOLOGETICALLY ME
'CAUSE THE TRUTH SET ME FREE!

CYPHERS
EVERYTHING YOU ARE
IS ABSOLUTELY, POSITIVELY, DEFINITELY
A-OKAY.
LIFE WILL TAKE YOU FAR
NO MATTER WHAT THE HATERS AND THE
PESSIMISTS SAY.

AIN'T NO QUESTION, YOU ARE THE ANSWER.
AIN'T NO LIMIT TO THE THINGS YOU DO, YOU
DO.
AIN'T NO QUESTION, YOU ARE THE ANSWER.
DON'T FORGET THE MAGIC LIVES IN YOU.

YOU ARE ENOUGH, ENOUGH.
YOU ARE ENOUGH, ENOUGH.

PRINCE
KEEP ON, AND YA DON'T STOP!

CYPHERS
YOU ARE ENOUGH, ENOUGH.
YOU ARE ENOUGH, ENOUGH.

PRINCE
KEEP ON, AND YA DON'T STOP!

SO THE MORAL OF THE STORY IS:
YOU CAN'T BE SCARED OF BEING GLORIOUS.
BE MYSELF, AIN'T NOTHIN' WRONG WITH
PRINCE!

PRINCE (CONT)

DON'T BE SCARED TO JUMP IF IT ALL MAKES
SENSE.
KEEP IT REAL AND FREE YOUR STYLE.
TAKE YA BAD SITUATION AND FLIP IT AROUND.
CAN'T BE A QUITTER IF YOU WANNA BE A
WINNER,
NO MATTER WHAT HAPPENS, ALWAYS
REMEMBER...

CYPHERS

EVERYTHING YOU ARE
IS ABSOLUTELY, POSITIVELY, DEFINITELY
A-OKAY.
LIFE WILL TAKE YOU FAR
NO MATTER WHAT THE HATERS AND THE
PESSIMISTS SAY.

AIN'T NO QUESTION, YOU ARE THE ANSWER.
AIN'T NO LIMIT TO THE THINGS YOU DO, YOU
DO.
AIN'T NO QUESTION, YOU ARE THE ANSWER.
DON'T FORGET THE MAGIC LIVES IN YOU.

YOU ARE ENOUGH, ENOUGH.

PRINCE

EVERYBODY GO AND CLAP FOR YOURSELF.
EVERYBODY GO AND CLAP FOR YOURSELF.
YOU DONE MADE IT THROUGH THE STORM
THIS FAR,
GO AND CLAP FOR YOURSELF.

CYPHERS

YOU'RE AMAZING!

PRINCE
WHY DON'T YOU CLAP FOR YOURSELF.

CYPHERS
YOU'RE BEAUTIFUL!

PRINCE
GO 'HEAD AND CLAP FOR YOURSELF!

CYPHERS
YOU'RE WONDERFUL!

PRINCE
GO 'HEAD AND CLAP FOR YOURSELF!

CYPHERS
YOU'RE MAGIC!

PRINCE
WHY DON'T YOU CLAP FOR YOURSELF!

CYPHERS
BLACK MAGIC!

PRINCE
GO 'HEAD AND CLAP FOR YOURSELF!

CYPHERS
EVERYTHING YOU ARE
IS ABSOLUTELY, POSITIVELY, DEFINITELY
A-OKAY.
LIFE WILL TAKE YOU FAR
NO MATTER WHAT THE HATERS AND THE
PESSIMISTS SAY.

AIN'T NO QUESTION, YOU ARE THE ANSWER.
AIN'T NO LIMIT TO THE THINGS YOU DO, YOU
DO.
AIN'T NO QUESTION, YOU ARE THE ANSWER.
DON'T FORGET THE MAGIC LIVES IN YOU.

YOU ARE ENOUGH, ENOUGH.
YOU ARE ENOUGH, ENOUGH.
YOU ARE ENOUGH, ENOUGH.
YOU ARE ENOUGH, ENOUGH.
YOU ARE ENOUGH, ENOUGH.
YOU ARE ENOUGH, ENOUGH.
YOU ARE ENOUGH, ENOUGH.
YOU ARE ENOUGH, ENOUGH.

(Everyone exits. PRINCE shares a moment with THE MC. PRINCE exits. THE MC holds up the Rhyme Book and closes it shut.)

BLACKOUT.

END OF SHOW.